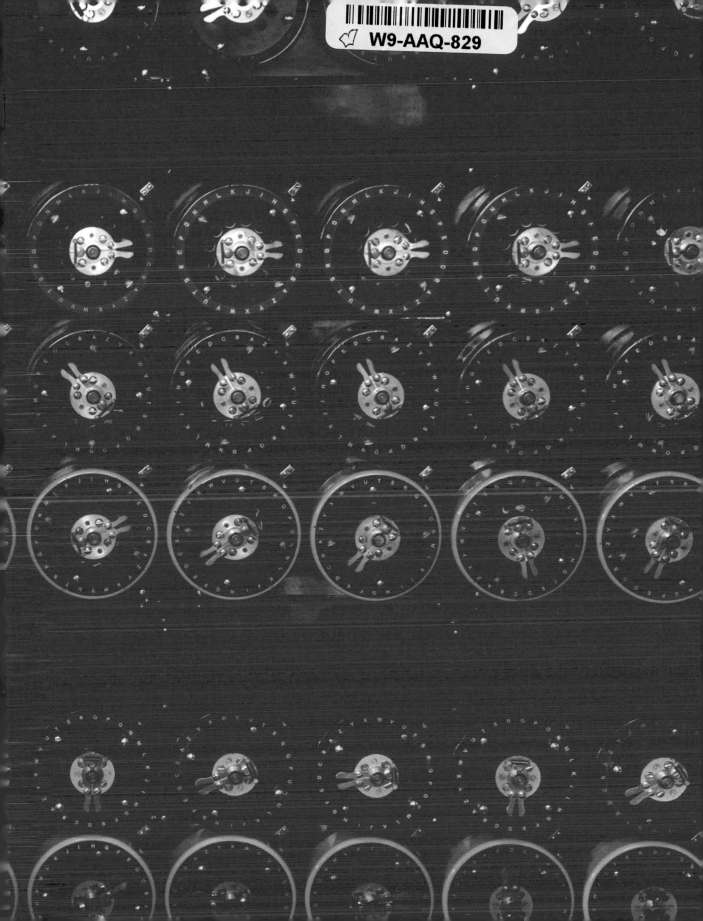
W9-AAQ-829

ENIGMA

HOW BREAKING THE CODE HELPED WIN WORLD WAR II

ENIGMA

HOW BREAKING THE CODE
HELPED WIN WORLD WAR II

MICHAEL KERRIGAN

amber
BOOKS

Copyright © 2018 Amber Books Ltd

Published by Amber Books Ltd
United House
London N7 9DP
United Kingdom
www.amberbooks.co.uk
Appstore: itunes.com/apps/amberbooksltd
Facebook: www.facebook.com/amberbooks
Twitter: @amberbooks

All rights reserved. With the exception of quoting brief passages for the purpose
of review no part of this publication may be reproduced without prior written
permission from the publisher. The information in this book is true and complete
to the best of our knowledge. All recommendations are made without any guarantee
on the part of the author or publisher, who also disclaim any liability incurred
in connection with the use of this data or specific details.

ISBN: 978-1-78274-587-7

Project Editor: Michael Spilling
Designer: Jerry Williams
Picture Researcher: Terry Forshaw

Printed in China

Picture Credits
Alamy: 9 (Rolf Richardson), 10 (Maurice Savage), 13 (The Print Collector), 22 (Stuart Robertson), 23 (Zuma Press),
    24 (Karen Fuller), 31 (Granger Collection), 36 (Ken Hawkins), 37 (PJF Military Collection), 38 (Bax Walker), 39
    (Famouspeople), 40 (A F Archive), 43 (Tony Rusecki), 46 (Bletchley Park – Andrew Nicholson), 51 (Hera Vintage
    Ads), 53 (Interfoto), 60 bottom (Zuma), 65 (Paul Fearn), 74 (Antiqua Print Gallery), 81 (Granger Collection), 85
    (HIP/Print Collector), 87 (World History Archive), 99 (Brian Harris), 122 (World History Archive), 129 (John Frost
    Newspapers), 137 (Keystone Pictures USA), 175 (Moviestore Collection), 177 (Prisma by Dukas Pressagentur GmbH),
    179 (Robert Evans), 180 (Ian Miles-Flashpoint Pictures), 184 (Granger Collection), 186 (Louis Berk), 187 (John Frost
    Newspapers), 193 (Jeff Gilbert), 200 (John Frost Newspapers), 201 (United Archives), 219 (Pictorial Press)
Art-Tech: 54, 56/57, 60 top, 61, 66, 70, 71, 72, 82, 89, 90, 120, 124, 126, 130, 131, 134/135, 141, 144, 145, 151, 157, 161,
    183, 192, 194, 195, 216/217
Cody Images: 26, 32, 63, 64, 73, 88, 91, 93–97 all, 103–105 all, 114–116 all, 118, 119, 127, 133, 140, 152, 154, 159, 160,
    162–167 all, 171, 197, 198, 203–206 all, 210, 211
Dreamstime: 6 (Gordon Bell), 33 (DVMS Images)
Mary Evans Picture Library: 76 & 77 (Illustrated London News), 78 (John Frost Newspapers)
Fotolia: 168
Getty Images: 8 (SSPL), 14 (Hulton/Simon Dack), 15 (Fox Photos), 18 (Hulton/Peter King), 48 (Anadalou Agency), 52
    (DEA/G. Nimatallah), 84 (Hulton), 106 (LIFE Picture Collection/James Jarche), 108 (Photo 12), 112 (Imperial War
    Museum), 117 (Planet News Archive), 147 (Popperfoto), 149 (Corbis), 153 & 156 (SSPL), 173 (Hulton), 190 (AFP),
    196 (Popperfoto), 209 (Hulton), 215 (Mondadori Portfolio), 220 (WPA/Arthur Edwards)
Getty/SSPL/Bletchley Park Trust: 16, 19–21 all, 41, 42, 55, 111, 142, 143, 185
Magnus Manske: 44 (Licensed under CC By-SA 3.0)
Public Domain: 28–30 all, 34, 35, 59, 79, 170, 174, 178, 208, 213
Shutterstock: 7 (Gavran 333), 25 (Wally Stemberger), 47 (Neftali), 100 (Mubus 7)
U.S. Department of Defense: 49, 101, 188
William Warby: 12

Contents

INTRODUCTION

CAPTAIN RIDLEY'S SHOOTING PARTY

No more improbable a set of heroes was ever assembled than the men and women brought together at Bletchley Park in 1938, but their work was to change the face of modern warfare.

'GARN, SMASH th' bastard! Garn, three inches in the throat! – Right nipple – left nipple – groin…'
Bayonet drill in basic training, as remembered by an old soldier of World War I in Henry Williamson's novella, *Love and the Loveless* (1958), leaves the new recruit in little doubt of what he faces in the field. The mud and gore; the blasts of the guns; the banshee wails of incoming shells and the shrieks of the wounded; the taste of cold steel and the smell of death…. All these impressions assault the fighter in the nightmare that is war.

If it isn't the savage intimacy of the killing – and the fear of dying, in all its gut-wrenching indignity – it's the sheer exhaustion of staying at one's post. For Lieutenant-Commander George Ericson, in Nicholas Monsarrat's novel of the Atlantic convoys, *The Cruel Sea* (1951), there's the all-but-obliterating stress of facing a 'gigantic sea' that sent 'solid tons of water' thundering down on the bridge about him, 'with a body from which every

Opposite: Big, but architecturally undistinguished, Bletchley Park could have been any of a thousand houses across the shires of provincial England.

Above: Bletchley railway station, 1950s. Bletchley railway station still exists, though the Oxford–Cambridge 'Varsity Line' doesn't – only a local line running east to Bedford.

instinct except dumb endurance had been drained.' In Randall Jarrell's famous poem, 'The Death of the Ball Turret Gunner' (1945), a US airman recalls soaring 'six miles from earth, loosed from its dream of life' before waking 'to black flak and the nightmare fighters'. 'When I died,' he concludes, 'they washed me out of the turret with a hose.'

A vast and varied modern literature has guaranteed that the most homebound of us has at least some appreciation of the realities of combat; some sense that, in the words of General William T. Sherman (1820–91), 'war is hell'.

PEACE AND QUIET

You couldn't get much further from the battlefront than the Bletchley Park of the 1930s. Set, as its name suggests, in leafy and expansive grounds, this big and sprawling English country house had been built by a wealthy architect and property developer in the nineteenth century. Despite these origins, the house was generally deemed at best undistinguished in its appearance, at worst a 'maudlin and monstrous Victorian pile'. With so little to offer in the way of aesthetic – and virtually nothing in dynastic – interest, it could hardly be counted among England's 'stately homes'. But if its beauties and its historical heritage might be disputed, the peace that prevailed here could not. A sleepier place and gentler pace of living would be hard to find.

THIS IS WAUGH...

Bletchley Park seemed the perfect place for the kind of elegantly accoutred country house gathering that, even in the 1930s, seemed to belong more obviously to a novel by Evelyn Waugh or P.G. Wodehouse than to real life. Brideshead was yet to be – Waugh would not publish his most famous novel until 1945 – but the Hetton Abbey of *A Handful of Dust* (1934) – a Victorian pile, described by the county guidebook as 'devoid of interest' – might readily have stood in for Bletchley Park. As for the engagingly blithering Bertie Wooster and his valet, Jeeves, they'd been delighting readers on both sides of the Atlantic for decades, but no one was in danger of confusing their comic milieu with real life.

YOU COULDN'T GET MUCH FURTHER FROM THE BATTLEFRONT THAN THE BLETCHLEY PARK OF THE 1930s.

Even now, the cover under which a group of young men and women converged on Bletchley Park from 14 August 1938 – that of 'Captain Ridley's Shooting Party' – seemed to stretch credulity a little. For one thing, the guests were not the obvious upper-class 'huntin', shootin', fishin' types. The odd shy stranger, cardboard suitcase in hand, arriving at Bletchley Station; the occasional group of sheepish-looking visitors having lunch in the Shoulder of Mutton pub…. These ill-sorted incomers weren't posh enough for the world of Wodehouse or Waugh, but – in their donnish

Below: Looking across the lake to Block A, built between 1941 and 1942 to house the centre's Air and Naval Intelligence sections.

abstraction – they scarcely seemed equipped for the real world either. Fortunately, few observers even registered their arrival in this backwater.

It was to be here, however, and by these young men and women, that – by some accounts – World War II was won. The claim is contentious, of course. Those who fought at Kursk or Stalingrad might reasonably cavil; so might those who sailed with the Arctic Convoys, contested every dune of the Libyan desert or every inch of Okinawa. Even so, the activities of the codebreakers brought together at Bletchley and the mass of signals material interpreted under the general heading of the 'Ultra Secret' were undoubtedly pivotal. As Churchill's 'most secret source', they illuminated almost every aspect of the Axis military effort (mostly Germany's and Italy's, but Japan's as well) and consequently informed almost every aspect of Allied strategy. Without their backroom work, the headline heroics could

Below: If the big house wasn't much to look at, the huts outside were still more anonymous: Bletchley Park was all about discretion.

MIDDLING MILTON KEYNES

RURAL BUCKINGHAMSHIRE lay at the very heart of the country – not just geographically, but culturally. With its well-tended fields, tidy woods and hedgerows and neatly laid-out villages, it approximated to a conventional ideal of Englishness. But the 'green and pleasant land' has been viewed more sceptically by postwar observers, for whom the idea of 'middle England' has been associated with unimaginative conformism and mediocrity.

The postwar New Town of Milton Keynes, of which Bletchley today forms part, has in recent years been reduced to recruiting professional PR advisers to counter what it sees as unhelpful stereotyping of the place. Far from winning admiration, its grid-like circuitboard of a street plan, its auto-friendly, roundabout-rich traffic management, and its avowedly modernist urban architecture were to see Milton Keynes ironically celebrated as Britain's most boring town. (The utmost derision was reserved for the gesture made towards the place's rural past in the establishment of a herd of concrete cows.)

Not that the young families flocking to what has in the last few years been one of England's fastest-growing urban centres seem to have found Milton Keynes quite so unsupportable. But progress isn't necessarily picturesque. Who, after all, could have imagined that the quiet and unassuming industry of the assembled geeks at Bletchley would have had so immense an impact on the conduct of modern war?

hardly have taken place, from the Battle of the Atlantic to the Normandy Landings and the race to the Rhine. The air of peace here was paradoxical: Bletchley Park was to play a significant – and in many cases crucial – backstage role for all the main theatres of the war.

OUT OF THE WAY

Bletchley's qualifications as a military headquarters were not self-evident. Again paradoxically, that was its chief qualification for its task. At this time not much more than a glorified village in rural Buckinghamshire, it lay well outside London and the great industrial regions of the West Midlands and the North. It was also as far from the sea as was possible in England: whether

Opposite: Dorothy Hyson as audiences had seen her on Broadway and in the West End. At Bletchley Park she was just another employee.

Below: A battered typewriter on an even more battered desk; a cup of tea ... it might be any English office of the 1940s. Today, Bletchley has been renovated to show future generations their work during the war.

or not Britannia could truly be said to 'rule the waves' must have seemed the most academic of questions here. There was no important road junction or river crossing here; no commanding heights or vital supply routes to be protected. Bletchley's major claim to strategic significance was unprecedented, and on the face of it improbable: its convenience for the Oxford-to-Cambridge railway line.

SWOTS ON THE MARCH

England's ancient universities had contributed their share of officers to the military over many generations. Never, however, had they been as key to the country's war effort as they were to be now. And it wasn't the old-fashioned 'Varsity Man' – the fresh-faced, self-confident and personable cricket-playing paragon – who was coming to his country's rescue. That kind of public schoolboy might have been ideally suited to the leadership of troops on the ground in the colonies or on the Western Front.

Above: In founding Amnesty International, Peter Benenson lit a candle for freedom of thought and expression: but he had arguably done the same at Bletchley Park.

Many were to do great things in the different theatres of World War II. But the work that was done at Bletchley Park was to take modern warfare in a new direction. For that, a new kind of soldiering – and a new kind of soldier – would be required.

The Bletchley Park project was to bring about the triumph of what we might now call the 'geek' or the 'nerd'. The words didn't exist as yet, but the new breed of heroes were bookish, unworldly hobbledehoys. There were exceptions to the rule, but they had stereotypically steered clear of the games field as far as possible at school, and frequently held back from the wider social ruck. We might see them as 'brilliant' now, given their first class degrees, but their achievements didn't dazzle their contemporaries in college. They were, for the most part, striving instead for the self-consciously effortless superiority they saw represented in the 'Gentleman's Third'.

History has largely forgotten those gilded youths, although many served with courage and distinction through World War II and made important contributions to their country afterwards. But the Bletchley Park roll of honour reads like a *Who's Who* of luminaries, ranging from politicians like Roy Jenkins (1920– 2003) – destined to serve as Britain's Home Secretary and, a decade or so later, as President of the European Commission – to art historians such as T.S.R. Boase (1898–1974). John Chadwick (1920–98) was to go from decrypting German dispatches to deciphering the pre-Classical Cretan writing known as Linear B. Chicago-born Dorothy Hyson (1914–96) came to Bletchley Park from Broadway – and subsequently resumed her successful career acting on the West End stage. Peter Benenson (1921–2005) became a distinguished lawyer and human rights campaigner: he founded Amnesty International in 1961. Novelists, poets, musicians, historians, language scholars and economists abound. And that's before we turn to the more obviously mathematical, scientific and computer-related fields. Alan Turing (1912–54), widely acclaimed as the 'Father of Computer Science', is only the most celebrated of the 'techies' stationed here.

ALL ABOUT ASA

Asa Briggs (1921–2016) wasn't just another veteran of Bletchley Park: he was to embody both its values and its legacy. An engineer's son from Keighley, West Yorkshire, he had won a place at Sidney Sussex College, Cambridge, to read history. Why, however, confine himself to so narrow an academic focus? Pretty much a one-man university, Briggs found time to study for an external degree from London. In 1941, he graduated with firsts in both.

That he was clever was obvious. But it was the breadth of his intellectual engagement that equipped him so well for life at Bletchley Park, where he served from 1942 to 1945. In the postwar period, he played an important part in the foundation of the University of Sussex (1961). At its opening, he was simultaneously its Professor of History and Dean of its School of Social Studies. The presence of one man in two such important positions reflected the new university's conscious attempt to offer 'interdisciplinary' approaches to learning, transcending the traditional demarcations between what were supposedly 'different' fields of study – but that actually involved important common strands.

But Briggs was interested in breaking social boundaries, too. If, as Provost of Worcester College, Oxford (1976–91), he occupied a place at the heart of England's academic establishment, his work as Chancellor of the Open University (1978–94) encouraged access to higher education for students from all social backgrounds who had missed life-transforming opportunities under the existing system.

Those achievements and that lustre lay some years – or even decades – in the future. At this stage, the Bletchley Boys weren't stars. Gauche and awkward, and sorely lacking in the firm, manly handshake department, those who ended up here had often been seen as the runts of the public-school litter. That's if they'd even been to public (in Britain, of course, that means 'private') school, for they came disproportionately from lower-middle-class provincial backgrounds and had received their education prior to university as charitably-assisted 'scholarship boys' at their local grammar schools. Regional accents – then, even more than now, seen as socially as well as geographically identifying – proclaimed their backgrounds to all who heard them speak. Thanks in part to their achievements here, a later generation would look back and romanticize – even revere – them for these modest origins. But at the time this kind of background was not something to be worn with pride.

Below: Women (here in Hut 3) undertook much of the daily grind at Bletchley Park, their work often boring – but extremely exacting.

A FAR CRY FROM KENSINGTON

THE NOW-CURIOUS CONVENTION by which the upper-class English girl was directed to a Swiss finishing school to acquire sophistication and social polish furnished Bletchley Park with several otherwise improbable recruits. Jane Fawcett (1921–2016), for one: this ballet-dancer *manquée* was back in London preparing to 'come out' into society, making her *début* at court, when she found an immensely welcome sanctuary in Hut 6. The German she'd learned at Zurich and St Moritz, rather than lending lustre to her self-presentation at exclusive *soirées*, helped her unpick the coded meaning of German signals. Most famously, they enabled her to establish the whereabouts of the battleship *Bismarck*, a prestigious prize, sunk by the Royal Navy on 27 May 1941. All in a day's work to Jane Fawcett and her colleagues, but a major coup – the first one, really – for the codebreaking operation at Bletchley Park.

AMONGST WOMEN

It is significant that at Bletchley Park these men were to find themselves so much in the company of women. It was to become a perk (and led to many a flirtation – even a few marriages) in time. But it wasn't the norm for a fighting force. Women, important as their ancillary role in combat as nurses, drivers, mechanics and secretarial aides might be, couldn't hope to play the crucial role they were in many cases doing here. Although the Soviet Union was to have its well-publicized (and genuinely influential) female fighter pilots and partisan infantry, British women were begrudged their place on the battlefield. Hence the excitement felt by so many of the 'Bletchley Girls', given their own chance of making history – albeit secretly. Even so, their presence at Bletchley Park, as clearly as it enhanced the centre's work with hindsight, would have seemed to subtly lower the status of its men.

In the event, the sexual politics of Bletchley Park were little different from those of a civilian office of the time: the women did repetitive, routine work, comparatively unskilled (though in many ways deeply demanding), while men had more

'MEANING-MAKING', FICTION-FAKING

CHRISTINE BROOKE-ROSE (1923–2012) WAS born in Geneva and brought up bilingual in French and English and a graduate of Somerville College, Oxford, and University College, London. After her wartime service at Bletchley Park, she made an important career as a writer – though her fiction, if admired, was not widely loved. She was unabashedly a 'difficult' writer; her novels were radically experimental in their treatment of language, time and plot. She thought conventional fiction could only reflect conventions: her work sought to strip out the cliché and get behind the guff.

Accordingly, *Between* (1968) got by without any use of the verb 'to be', *Next* (1998) without the verb 'to have'. In *Xorandor* (1986), the narration is conducted by a pair of twins typing at a computer in their own self-developed techno-slang. This sort of serious play with established narrative norms was familiar to readers of such Modernist writers as James Joyce and Ezra Pound, but it was also the codebreaker's stock in trade. At Bletchley Park, Brooke-Rose had a unique insight into what she saw as the inadequacy of our modern ways of 'meaning-making' and the catastrophic consequences this could have.

In *Remake* (1996), Brooke-Rose wrote an autobiography without the first-person 'I' in which she recalled what the 'Old Lady' had learnt from her years at Bletchley Park. 'The otherness of the other learnt young, the real war, seen from the enemy

Christine Brooke-Rose (centre) was to draw on her Bletchley Park experiences in her writing.

point of view ... intercepted, decrypted, translated and transmuted.' This, she had come to realize, was the very essence of her inspiration – and in a way it is surely what any serious author seeks to do. She retained to the last the assumption, gained at Bletchley Park, that writing was as much about concealment as it was communication. Was it wry self-deprecation or a deeper philosophical scepticism that made her tell one interviewer that she felt a sense of freedom as a writer from knowing that no one would read her works?

managerial and 'creative' roles. Given that these women were also often highly educated, graduates of the great universities themselves, and with a corresponding self-confidence and sense of entitlement, resentments could be felt and sparks could sometimes fly. Yet even drudgery at Bletchley Park presented stimulating challenges – and, as the war went on and they saw their efforts pay off in far-off fields and seas, all could share the sense of pride in being involved in such important work.

WHITE-COLLAR WARFARE

Snobbery and sexism are both irritating; they can cumulatively be demoralizing – but this is hardly the stuff of Stalingrad or Midway. What's a little condescension beside the life-and-death dangers encountered daily on the battlefront? What were *any* of the trials the Bletchley workers faced? Lousy food; long hours of often dreary (but still pressured) work; inadequate heating; infestations of mice in sleeping accommodation … none of these problems was exactly life-threatening.

Bletchley Park was to see some real action, though: three bombs hit the site, doing damage to Hut 4, one night in November 1940 – though even they seem to have been aimed at Bletchley's railway station.

Below: Staff in Hut 6's registration room sorted out coded intercepts (by frequency and call-sign), as they came in.

When we try to assess the Bletchley Park achievement, or understand the stresses its staff contended with, we get no help from the traditional templates of military history, or, at a more personal level, those of conventional military memoir. Service at Bletchley Park was more about number crunching than square bashing; about decrypting and reading messages than rifle drill. The risks were not of dying but of missing vital data – or of decrypting it too late. The unrelenting pressure involved may

seem trivial beside the terror of the soldier, seaman or airman under fire – and, objectively it was. But it was unrelenting pressure nonetheless.

BEFORE ITS TIME

In the comedy movie *21 Jump Street* (2012), two young-looking police officers are sent to work undercover in an American high school to investigate a drug-dealing ring. One, Greg Jenko (Channing Tatum), was in his day a dim and academically idle but sportingly – and socially – successful 'jock'. As such, he can now look back complacently at a glorious career as teenage royalty, while his colleague Morton Schmidt (Jonah Hill) dreads returning to the living hell that high school was for him. In the event, Morton fits right in, his intelligence and sensitivity warmly appreciated by his new 'contemporaries'. They are at best bewildered by Greg's idle assurance, and – wrapped up in their own fashionable enthusiasms and subcultures – unimpressed by his attainments on the track.

It's been a bit like that for Bletchley Park. Not that its contribution could be said to be unappreciated: there were

Below: Information from decrypted transcripts was kept on indexed punch-cards in Block C's file room – now the visitors' reception at Bletchley Park.

obvious and excellent reasons for the secrecy with which its work was surrounded during the war and well into the Cold War era. Even so, the way that work has caught the popular imagination since the first revelations started appearing in the 1970s seem to reflect important changes through this time. Had wartime Britain been told of these achievements, would it even have been equipped to understand them? Would later generations, well into the postwar years? It's hard to imagine that they would. Few could have understood the technical questions involved, even fewer the free-ranging creativity that was harnessed here.

Above: Hut 6's Intercept Control Room kept up contact with the wireless stations round the country from where the coded signals came.

A HIPSTER HISTORIOGRAPHY

Bletchley Park and its men and women have become recent history's Morton Schmidt. Alan Turing seems like our contemporary now in a way he never could to his own generation – tragically, in his sexuality; intellectually, in what we'd call his Information Technology (IT) skills. His name is known to a generation who might struggle to identify such sometime-icons as Winston Churchill, Field Marshals Montgomery and Rommel or General Eisenhower. And that's understandable.

Above: Getting on for 150 people worked in Hut 8 decrypting German naval signals – a particularly productive source of ULTRA information.

In the most narrowly technical sense, signals intelligence (SIGINT) has become central to modern spycraft; computer science key to just about every aspect of arms technology and defence design. The defining weapon of our times, the drone, represents the culminating triumph of 'white-collar warfare', directed from a remote 'backroom' directly to the frontline.

These developments in the military sphere reflect the growing importance of IT in modern life more widely. Skills developed at Bletchley Park have spilled into every area of existence now: computers, email, online databases; 'smart' technology from phones and fridges to auto engines and central-heating systems; the Internet, and all that's come with it, from up-to-the-second news updates to social media, from clickbait journalism to bootleg music streaming.

BACK TO REALITY

So fascinating is the story of Bletchley Park, so vast its postwar legacy, that we can forget that this great social and cultural experiment actually came with a war attached. Understandably, given the creativity it unleashed and its continuing topicality, it is viewed as a particularly upbeat episode of Britain's recent past. But that emblematic drone, no matter how sophisticated its computerized launch and guidance systems, will still hit a target somewhere – and when it does, it is with old-fashioned explosive force. However meticulous the preparation, however accurate the targeting, however 'surgical' the strike, we're back with the violence of the blast and the hell of war. It was just the same in World War II: all the brains in the world weren't going to reason Nazi Germany out of its racially directed expansionism or Imperial Japan out of its colonialist aggression in the East.

Ultimately, the point of Bletchley Park was the defence of Britain and its allies and the defeat of its Axis enemies. Both these tasks had to be accomplished in the real world. The purpose of this book is not to diminish the wider significance of the Bletchley Park project, but to renew focus on its original wartime role – its impact in the field of battle and its implications for the war by air and sea. Real orders were issued, real plans were hatched, on the strength of intelligence from Bletchley Park.

The intelligence known collectively as 'Ultra' strengthened the hand of the Allied command immeasurably. So powerful a capability did it give them that, paradoxically, they had to exercise great care in using it so as not to betray their possession of it to the enemy. Hence the unexpected challenge of having to 'play God': some engagements might have been deliberately lost; some possessions consciously written off for fear of showing their hand too plainly to the Germans.

Below: Operatives actually listened in on enemy transmissions using this equipment. Increasingly, though, Bletchley Park relied on 'Y-stations' situated elsewhere.

1

UNLOCKING ENIGMA

The establishment of Bletchley Park was also the culmination of years of pre-war work attempting to unpick a new and devilishly difficult generation of German codes.

PERHAPS NO single fact proclaims more eloquently the innovative nature of the Bletchley Park achievement than the leading role played by Alfred Dillwyn 'Dilly' Knox (1884–1943). A Fellow of King's College, Cambridge, he was indisputably a hero, but of a kind unprecedented in military history. An alpha male only in the thoroughness of his grounding in Greek script, the closest thing he had to a war wound was the damage he'd done to his eyesight poring over papyrus scripts by the poet Herodas of Alexandria (third century BCE). Fulfilling the absent-minded professor stereotype to a T, he was once observed by an assistant trying to stuff a sandwich into his pipe instead of his tobacco.

Knox might have been an unlikely warrior, but he'd already served his country during World War I. From the start of hostilities, he had worked at cracking German naval codes in Room 40 – the centre for cryptanalysis for the British forces – in the Admiralty's Old Building, in Whitehall, London. The name

Opposite: The Bombe's 36 revolving drums allowed it to run through all the possible permutations of the Enigma machine's three rotors at some speed.

is additionally significant, reminding us that cryptography was still so marginal an activity in military intelligence that all its operatives could be quartered comfortably in a single room.

Work in Room 40 was mostly organized around the Imperial German Navy's *Signalbuch der Kaiserlichen Marine,* or 'SKM', a copy of which had been retrieved by the Russians from a sinking German cruiser. A copy of the *Handelsschiffsverkehrsbuch* – the codebook used by merchant vessels and U-boats – subsequently added a new dimension of understanding. Further finds offered fresh illumination: in all, the Room 40 workers were to read around 15,000 German communications.

A TIPPING POINT?

Some of the coded communications were more important than others. Knox's decryption of the 'Zimmermann Telegram' (1917) was a case in point. This missive, named for the German foreign minister who had authored it, invited Mexico to ally with Berlin, isolating Washington. Its interception and exposure represented a real breakthrough for Britain diplomatically, helping precipitate the United States' entry into World War I.

How are we to assess the scale of Knox's achievement within the wider context of the conflict? Others (in their hundreds of

Below: It was the sinking of a Magdeburg-class cruiser that allowed the Russians to secure the German naval codebook for World War I.

OLIVER!

LYTTON STRACHEY (1880–1932) has gone down in literary history as a sort of small-time Oscar Wilde, yet there was nothing small about his reputation in his time. At Cambridge, a member of the assertively elitist Apostles society (only twelve undergraduates at a time were allowed to be members), he showed a flair for provocative publicity-seeking as an advocate of what he called 'Higher Sodomy'. He was hardly less notorious afterwards as a friend of Virginia Woolf and a founder member of the Bloomsbury Group of writers, artists and thinkers.

Meanwhile, whether driven into unwilling obscurity in his younger brother's slipstream or availing himself of the cover it provided, Oliver Strachey (1874–1960) was beavering away in the bowels of Whitehall, breaking codes. He remained in the Government Code and Cipher School between the wars, and was a natural choice to help set up operations at Bletchley Park. He wasn't without his own artistic side, as a keen pianist, or even an anti-establishment streak: his wife Rachel 'Ray' Strachey (née Costelloc) was an important feminist campaigner and pamphleteer. That maverick side must have come in handy in his dealings with double agents: Strachey was to command his own ISOS ('Intelligence Service Oliver Strachey') within the wider operation at Bletchley Park.

thousands) were enduring the infernal conditions of the fighting front: the cold, the wet, the mud, the rats, the lice – let alone the small-arms fire and the falling shells. Knox never had to go 'over the top' to just-about-certain death; nor did he have to see a comrade die before his eyes. But the significance of his achievement, objectively speaking, outweighs even the noblest battlefield heroics, however much he would have admired and respected those.

TECHNOLOGICAL ADVANCE

Codebreaking called for skills of hard reasoning and logic of the highest order, but what we might see as 'softer' intuitions and insights could be important too. Another of Knox's early triumphs had been his speed in spotting that a certain cryptographer at the German admiralty was using snatches of Romantic poetry as the basis for his codes. But if there was always a place for inspiration in codebreaking, perspiration was becoming more important as the volume and complexity of coded messages increased.

Although espionage was as old as warfare, it had been given institutional status in Britain (as MI6 – and, for counter-espionage, MI5) as recently as 1909. And while the use of codes could not have been much younger, the kind of hand-ciphers that had been the norm until now had meant messages being sent – and, where intercepted, interpreted – locally. The advent of mechanical aids in the early years of the twentieth century opened the way to cryptography, and cryptanalysis, on a larger scale. If you could have a typewriter, why not a typewriter-with-a-twist, changing letters to a pre-established formula? If you could have an adding machine, why not one primed to modify entered numbers further, following a predetermined code?

Keeping pace with technological improvements in other areas (this was the age of the submarine, the aeroplane and the tank, among other innovations), codemaking and -breaking were both developing in scale and speed – and, consequently, in strategic significance. There was no question of Room 40's work ending with the Armistice in 1918, though it was to move its headquarters within Whitehall and change its name. As of the end of 1919, as the

Below: The deciphering of the 'Zimmermann Telegram' changed the entire course of World War I, triggering the United States' decision to join the conflict.

WESTERN UNION TELEGRAM

NEWCOMB CARLTON, PRESIDENT

Send the following telegram, subject to the terms on back hereof, which are hereby agreed to

via Galveston

JAN 19 1917

GERMAN LEGATION

MEXICO CITY

130	13042	13401	8501	115	3528	416	17214	6491	11310
18147	18222	21560	10247	11518	23677	13605	3494	14936	
98092	5905	11311	10392	10371	0302	21290	5161	39695	
23571	17504	11269	18276	18101	0317	0228	17694	4473	
23284	22200	19452	21589	67893	5569	13918	8958	12137	
1333	4725	4458	5905	17166	13851	4458	17149	14471	6706
13850	12224	6929	14991	7382	15857	67893	14218	36477	
5870	17553	67893	5870	5454	16102	15217	22801	17138	
21001	17388	7446	23638	18222	6719	14331	15021	23845	
3156	23552	22096	21604	4797	9497	22464	20855	4377	
23610	18140	22260	5905	13347	20420	39689	13732	20667	
6929	5275	18507	52262	1340	22049	13339	11265	22295	
10439	14814	4178	6992	8784	7632	7357	6926	52262	11267
21100	21272	9346	9559	22464	15874	18502	18500	15857	
2188	5376	7381	98092	16127	13486	9350	9220	76036	14219
5144	2831	17920	11347	17142	11264	7667	7762	15099	9110
10482	97556	3569	3670						

BERNSTORFF.

Charge German Embassy.

Government Code and Cypher School (GC&CS), it was to work unceasingly and on a growing scale, monitoring signals traffic, and refining its interception and protection skills.

INTERPRETING HISTORY

At the head of GC&CS was another Room 40 veteran, Alastair Denniston (1881–1961). A brilliant codebreaker, he was also an insightful reader of his times. Not only did Denniston see before many of his contemporaries the reality that cryptography would only grow in importance, he was also quick in appreciating the Nazi threat.

In response to his perceptions of this mounting danger, he put out feelers through the 1930s, sounding out academic contacts about young students of promise. This was how he discovered Bristol-born mathematician Gordon Welchman (1906–85), then a Fellow of Sidney Sussex College, Cambridge, and brought him into GC&CS. Welchman would in turn recruit another young maths genius: his chess-playing partner from Cambridge, Stuart Milner-Barry (1906–95). Milner-Barry had been working as a stockbroker since leaving college, but maintained his friendship with Welchman, and his interest in chess: he competed internationally, refining the thinking skills that would stand him in such good stead in cracking code.

Milner-Barry subsequently brought his Cambridge friend Hugh Alexander (1909–74) into the Bletchley fold: a fellow chess player, he'd been teaching maths

Below: The decrypted 'Zimmermann Telegram' could hardly have been clearer in its implications. As its author admitted, its leaking made war with America 'certain'.

TELEGRAM RECEIVED.

FROM 2nd from London # 5747.

"We intend to begin on the first of February unrestricted submarine warfare. We shall endeavor in spite of this to keep the United States of America neutral. In the event of this not succeeding, we make Mexico a proposal of alliance on the following basis: make war together, make peace together, generous financial support and an understanding on our part that Mexico is to reconquer the lost territory in Texas, New Mexico, and Arizona. The settlement in detail is left to you. You will inform the President of the above most secretly as soon as the outbreak of war with the United States of America is certain and add the suggestion that he should, on his own initiative, invite Japan to immediate adherence and at the same time mediate between Japan and ourselves. Please call the President's attention to the fact that the ruthless employment of our submarines now offers the prospect of compelling England in a few months to make peace." Signed, ZIMMERMANN.

The receipt of this information has so greatly exercised the British Government that they have lost no time in communicating it to me to transmit to you, in order that our Government may be able without delay to make such disposition as may

Above: As head of GC&CS, Alastair Denniston was responsible for bringing together the team that worked such wonders at Bletchley Park.

at Winchester College, one of England's most famous public schools. Alexander was actually in Buenos Aires, Argentina, representing England in the Chess Olympiad, when World War II broke out: he hastily withdrew and headed back to Bletchley.

Milner-Barry also recruited several women. 'I lived in Cambridge', he later recalled, 'and had the advantage of a close connection with Newnham College, where my sister Ada had been Vice-Principal until her untimely death in 1938. So I was able to recruit a few girls from both Newnham and Girton Colleges....' Ada Milner-Barry had been a literary scholar researching eighteenth-century poets such as Oliver Goldsmith. But she too did her bit for the war effort, passing on the names of promising students she had taught or heard about from her fellow academics: such were the ways of recruitment at Bletchley Park.

OLD SCHOOL TIES?

This kind of contact, along an informal 'old-boy' (and 'old-girl') network, would come under increasingly critical scrutiny in postwar Britain. It has been seen as at best a source of social division and resentment, at worst the dismal driver of a class-bound country's economic decline. It's anti-transparent, critics say; not just unfair but reactionary, keeping power and influence in the hands of those who've always held it.

These criticisms can't easily be dismissed. All we can say of Alastair Denniston and his networking is that it was driven by a different logic, and that the eventual end was to justify the means. The reality is that Oxford and Cambridge were at that time Britain's main – and maybe only real – habitat for the kind of quirky, restless, brilliant mind he sought. And personal connection was the only practicable way of finding the right kind of character: Denniston needed a certain type of person – quick and compulsively curious – not a set of qualifications.

If GC&CS grew organically, that was surely because it had to: the strict discipline that ruled other departments of government service would have smothered its creativity at birth. By military standards shockingly anarchic (one arrival was taken aback by the blank stare his new boss greeted him with when he saluted), the culture at GC&CS and at Bletchley Park lent itself to risk-taking and innovative thought.

But those risks had to be taken, those innovative thoughts had to be explored in a context of complete loyalty and trust. Noting that no fewer than twelve dons were brought to Bletchley Park from King's College, Cambridge alone, historian Hilary Footitt argues that the reasons for this bias went well beyond IQ. The authorities didn't just value the maverick brilliance of the best

INTELLECTUAL BABBAGE

THE LEADING SPIRITS of Bletchley Park did not for the most part represent the highest social echelons – the men, especially, were mainly 'local boys made good'. But another Cambridge friend of Gordon Welchman's, his fellow mathematician Dennis Babbage (1909–91), had certain claims to scientific aristocracy at least. Although he wasn't Dennis' direct ancestor, his relation Charles Babbage (1791–1871) had, with his Difference Engine, created in 1822, and the Analytical Engine he proposed in 1837, arguably invented the computer.

Right: Babbage's mechanization of maths was to have far-reaching implications. Here we see his 'Difference Engine' as originally designed.

Opposite: The three-rotor Enigma machine offered quick and easy encryption to a high level.

Below: Enigma goes into action in France with General Heinz Guderian (1888–1954). His *blitzkrieg* tactics demanded close radio contact with tank formations and air support.

Oxbridge thought but the collegiate spirit that underpinned it. Whatever their historic faults of elitism and social exclusivity, the ancient universities were genuine communities of the mind. Indulgent as they were to the original thinking of the individualist intellect, they saw learning as a collective endeavour overall.

As we've already seen, if recruitment here was open to the charge of cronyism, it was a cronyism that ignored the embedded English class values reigning elsewhere. Not that GC&CS' recruits were for the most part working class – this was what Karl Marx would have called a 'bourgeois revolution' – but they represented a radical departure nonetheless. Denniston was a doctor's son from Greenock, west Scotland; Gordon Welchman's father had been a vicar; Alexander's an engineering professor; Milner-Barry's a schoolteacher in suburban London.

By 1938, accordingly, when, as 'Captain Ridley', he came to organize his 'shooting party', Denniston could call upon the assistance of a motley – but mightily talented – young crew.

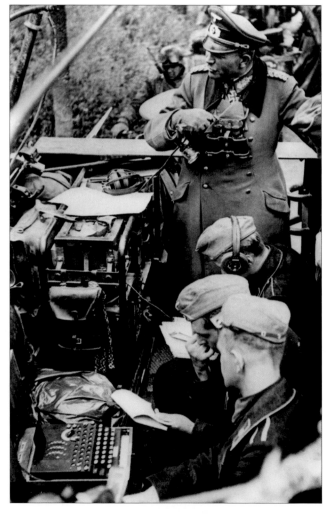

INTRODUCING ENIGMA
All this time, meanwhile, even though his own family had been kept in ignorance, Dilly Knox had never severed his connection with the security services. Indeed, under Denniston's auspices, he'd moved into a leading role behind the scenes. As the years went by and he worked away at his day job deciphering Greek-Egyptian papyri, he kept an eye on developments in cryptography.

It seems to have been Knox who bought Britain's first Enigma machine, after it was presented at the International Postal Union Congress

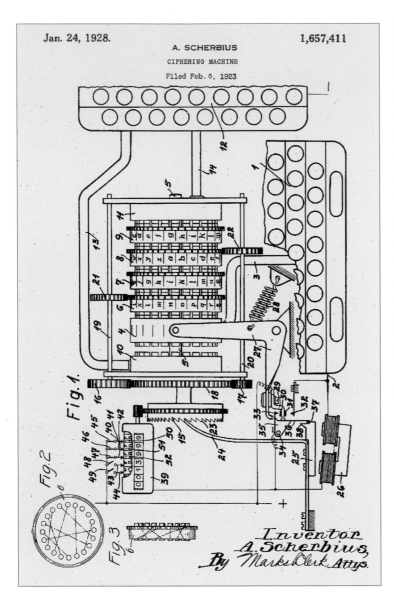

Jan. 24, 1928.

A. SCHERBIUS

1,657,411

CIPHERING MACHINE

Filed Feb. 6, 1923

Inventor
A. Scherbius,
By Marks Clerk Attys.

Above: Scherbius' patent form for what was eventually to become Enigma shows clearly how complex substitutions could be simply made.

in Switzerland in 1923. Designed by Arthur Scherbius (1878–1929), it featured a rotor cipher – a succession of concentrically arranged and numbered rotors or wheels with electronic contacts along a single axis that could be used to create complex yet consistent substitutions for each letter entered. Each wheel substituting the letters of the last according to a predetermined formula, Enigma introduced multiple layers of encryption automatically. Not only would code so comprehensively scrambled be difficult to decipher in the first place, the encryption code could be changed at a moment's notice.

Dutch inventors Theo van Hengel (1875–1939) and Rudolf Spengler (1875–1955) had devised something along these lines some years before, but Scherbius had been the first to make it work. German naval intelligence had shown an interest in early versions of Enigma since the end of World War I, but the machine had been refined since then for military – and now for commercial – use.

RINGING UP THE CHANGES
Serious codemakers could already venture far beyond the sort of simplistic A:1, B:2, C:3 substitutions small children at play might use for their secret messages – or the smarter A:2, B:3, C:4

substitutions they might think of when they were older. But even the most sophisticated cryptographers were limited in their scope by the lack of any quick and reliable way of recording the kind of complex substitution that could stand up to sustained analysis. This, however, was what the Enigma machine – ultimately a spin-off of the new generation of cash registers – could provide. With an Enigma machine at each end of the transmission – one to encrypt the message and the other to unpack it again – communications could be quick and security-robust.

But the inestimable advantage of Enigma wasn't just that it allowed more complex substitutions – no code, however complex, can be quite secure. Enigma allowed the substitutions used to be quickly and easily changed by prearrangement, so those trying to crack the code never had the time to get a real purchase. If these changes were to be carried out frequently and in a coordinated manner across as vast a cryptographic operation as the German military's, the chances of British codebreakers making appreciable inroads on their intelligence were next to none.

Snatches of Schiller or popular proverbs weren't going to cut it in this new cryptographical environment; nor would mastery of German service slang. GC&CS was going to be defeated both by the volume of encrypted traffic the new technology allowed and the speed with which the cipher could be changed. Of course, they could have Enigma themselves. Knox got his own machine simply by buying a commercial model in 1926. But this only gained him access to the field of play. It didn't offer any significant

Below: Theo van Hengel had beaten Scherbius to the thinking behind Enigma, but failed to find a way of making the whole thing work.

CIPHERS, HOWEVER COMPLEX, COME DOWN TO SIMPLE SUBSTITUTIONS: THIS LETTER STANDS FOR THAT ONE; THIS NUMBER FOR THAT OTHER ONE.

entry to the stream of coded communications passing back and forth on a daily, hourly basis along the wires.

Ciphers of this kind, however complex, in the end come down to simple substitutions: this letter stands for that one; this number for that other one. More sophisticated codes involved the replication, redoubling – and, ideally, much more – of such substitutions, building simple equivalences into elaborate and complex ones. Maddeningly laborious and time-consuming work, this was made much easier

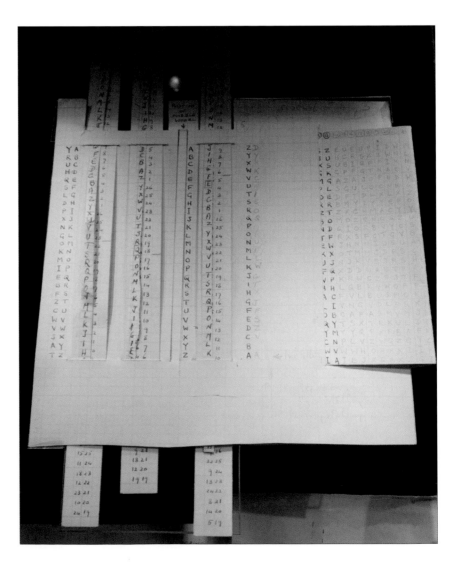

Right: Decoding sheets like this one were a handy way of trying out possible substitutions without the trouble of trawling through completely with a Bombe.

by the introduction of Enigma. Easier for Germany's cryptographers, that is: for GC&CS, it was a nightmare.

COMETH THE HOUR, COMETH THE CRYPTOGRAPHER

Enter Alan Turing (1912–54). A Londoner by birth – the son of a colonial official – he'd been brought up largely in St Leonard's-on-Sea in Sussex. After studying at Sherborne School, in Dorset, he'd gone to Cambridge to study maths – with such success that, in addition to gaining a first class degree, he won a fellowship at his college, King's. Even by Bletchley Park standards, Turing was extraordinarily gifted; he was extraordinarily troubled as well. His problems went back to his years at Sherborne.

Generations of young men could testify that the English public-school environment fostered close and intense male friendships. Homosocial bonding was routine, and some homosexual acts accepted. But Sherborne would have been no more sympathetic than society at large to a homosexual identity that went deeper. Homosexuality was seen as a sickness; a set of 'unnatural' and obscene acts. The idea that it might constitute an identity – and an acceptable one at that – was still pretty alien, even to homosexuals themselves. Self-hatred was often an inseparable part of being gay.

These general difficulties were in Turing's case heightened by the tragic death from tuberculosis of his closest school companion, Christopher Morcom, in 1930. Turing seems to have spent much of the next decade in deep mourning. However, he determined to honour his love for Christopher

Above: The codebreaker's notes handwritten on this February, 1945, message to Army Group Kurland make it clear that decryption was well advanced.

Opposite: His modern
fame may have meant
others' contributions being
unfairly marginalized, but
there's no disputing the
genius of Alan Turing.

Below: Turing's desk,
displayed at Bletchley
Park, reminds us of the
austerity amidst which
some of the greatest
advances of modern times
were made.

in the way he believed his friend would have wanted. 'I know I must put as much energy...into my work as if he were alive, because that is what he would like me to do,' Turing told his mother in a letter home.

Turing's brilliance and work ethic went together to produce outstanding results. He had set out the theoretical basis for a Universal Computing Machine by 1936. A PhD at Princeton followed, completed just two years later, in 1938, but he was back in Britain in time for the outbreak of the war. And, of course, for his invitation to 'Captain Ridley's Shooting Party'.

BLETCHLEY PARK TAKES SHAPE

Activities at Denniston's new headquarters at first centred on the big house itself. While MI6 had their offices hidden away upstairs, the regular sections for army, naval and air intelligence

had their own allocated spaces on the ground floor. There was also a little telephone exchange down here. But these quarters were all quickly filled, and staff and equipment had to be decanted into prefabricated wooden huts in the grounds outside.

To begin with, Hut 1 was the wireless centre: receivers for listening in to German radio broadcasts were placed here, though they were later concealed in a water tower on the estate. Hut 2 was a 'mess' for refreshments and relaxation; Hut 4 handled German naval intelligence; Hut 6 dealt with air-force communications; Hut 5 more general military intelligence relating to Italy and to European fellow-travellers such as

ALAN'S GIRL

AMONG STUART MILNER-BARRY'S Cambridge 'girls' was Newnham alumna Joan Clarke (1907–96). She was to follow her wartime cryptanalyst's career with important research into the history of Scottish coins. For non-numismatists, though, she's been of interest as the almost-Mrs Turing: they became engaged in 1941, though her fiancé finally decided he couldn't go through with their marriage. Afterwards, she admitted she had suspected his homosexuality long before he'd explicitly confided in her, but she had loved the close platonic friendship they had shared.

Turing seems to have treated Joan as an equal intellectual and emotional partner – perhaps his closest since Christopher Morcom – and that must have felt powerfully affirming for her. After all, this was a time when the authorities were – officially and unabashedly – paying women lower wages for doing the same work as

Above: Keira Knightley and Benedict Cumberbatch star as Joan and Alan in *The Imitation Game*.

their male colleagues. Whatever a life with Alan was going to lack from her perspective, his recognition of her right to be a thinking person must have felt genuinely bracing to Joan. A version of their relationship is the basis for the 2014 movie *The Imitation Game*.

Portugal and Spain. Hut 7 was for Japanese intelligence of all kinds. Oliver Strachey's OSIS had Huts 9 and 18 at its disposal.

As the war went on, and the operations expanded, these huts were supplemented by brick-built blocks. By the end of the war, several thousand men and women were working here.

OF PRACTICALITIES AND POLES

Turing was always going to be the star of Bletchley Park, even if his celebrity would have to be strictly local, barely extending beyond the walls of the big house. Not that his real fame would yet be warranted. His genius notwithstanding, the 'Turing Machine' didn't yet exist except in brilliant theory. One of the first tasks Turing faced when he arrived at Bletchley Park was to

Above: The machine room in Hut 6 was the beating heart of Bletchley Park: here women tried out code combinations in copies of Enigma.

Above: Work at Bletchley Park was progressively mechanized for greater scale and speed, giving the place the look and feel of an 'intelligence factory'.

come up with a way of realizing what he called his 'a machine' ('a' for automatic).

In the event, he approached his task obliquely. Bletchley Park wasn't an academic institution, after all. It had a well-defined job to do, and the exploration of computational theory wasn't it. The Turing Machine would have to wait. Instead, Turing was set to work trying to build on the practical progress made by others. British cryptographers weren't the only people who had been busy unpacking Enigma's secrets. Indeed, in important ways they lagged behind their Polish peers.

Assisted by their sources in French intelligence, who had passed on codebooks sold to them by the German spy Hans-Thilo Schmidt (1888–1943), the Poles had done a great deal of work on Enigma's functioning. Under the inspired leadership of the mathematician-cum-cryptologist Marian Rejewski (1905–80), they'd even built their own electro-mechanical 'key' to Enigma's workings: the *bomba kryptologiczna*. So-called because they hoped it would explode the secrecy of the Enigma codes? Some have suggested that. It was an impressive piece of work, effectively an attempt to reverse-engineer the workings of the Enigma machine, reproducing the logical processes by which its different rotors were selected, and so progressively unpicking the cryptographical makings of each code.

THE POLES HAD DONE A GREAT DEAL OF WORK ON ENIGMA'S FUNCTIONING. THEY'D EVEN BUILT THEIR OWN ELECTRO-MECHANICAL 'KEY' TO ENIGMA'S WORKINGS.

ENIGMA ENHANCED

In practice, the *bomba kryptologiczna* was not so much a 'bomb' as a damp squib, slow and cumbersome. It was fine as long as the Germans kept the volume of their communications low and were conveniently slack about the need to change their ciphers. However, every time the Germans changed their code, the *bomba*'s operators had to go back to first principles and reinvent the cryptanalytical wheel, running through a million possible permutations until the right ones had been found.

Fortunately for the Poles, changing ciphers was an administrative headache for the Germans too, involving coordination across all relevant branches of government and armed services. The temptation was always to procrastinate and let things lie. However, as the 1930s went on, the military situation grew more serious and German intelligence tightened up its procedures, the Polish *bomba* struggled to keep up. Then, with war around the corner, at the very end of 1938, the Germans radically upgraded their Enigma machines. The addition of two extra rotors, taking the total

Below: Polish cryptographer Marian Rejewski was to be a major figure in what might be called the 'prehistory' of Bletchley Park.

up to five, set the *bomba* an altogether more difficult challenge. By the time war was declared between Britain and Germany on 3 September 1939, the Enigma machine being used by German Naval Intelligence had eight rotors.

The beauty of the upgraded Enigma machine from the cryptographer's point of view was the incredible number of permutations it could provide, the multiple levels of encryption it could yield. It didn't end with the different combinations offered by the rotors: what was called a 'plugboard' enabled the operator to intervene manually, substituting one letter for another (anything up to ten times over at a time) in counterpoint with the substitutions being made automatically by the machine. This left anyone hoping to crack the code looking for the cryptological equivalent of a needle in a haystack. The possible permutations were just about infinite.

Or at least they would have seemed so to a lay observer. To the kind of minds assembled at Bletchley, they were simply vast. Again, the problem wasn't the complexity of the codes as such but the ease and frequency with which they could now be changed.

Left: The addition of a fourth rotor in 1938 made Enigma more formidable. Soon a fifth, a sixth … and ultimately an eighth, were added.

'ANYONE FOR TENNIS?'

BLETCHLEY PARK MIGHT HAVE been a cushy billet by the standards of the shooting war, but the work was hard and unrelenting nonetheless. Studying screeds of encrypted babble for hours on end; trying out endless different 'cribs' and combinations – for the most part fruitlessly – took a toll on the mental faculties over time. Some way of relaxing was essential, as Winston Churchill recognized when, on a visit to the site, he called for tennis courts to be constructed. Table tennis was already on offer at nearby Bletchley Senior School, its facilities made available to GC&CS staff.

As befits its Oxbridge antecedents, Bletchley Park had comparatively rarefied tastes in entertainment: the chess club was unsurprisingly well supported. So, too, were sports like fencing, along with more obviously cultural activities, from music recitals to reading in the library. But it was with their amateur theatricals that staff really made their splash. A hugely important aspect of Oxbridge student life, the dramatic passion was imported wholesale to Bletchley Park: light-entertainment shows with comic skits and songs, and more serious plays from Shakespeare to George Bernard Shaw.

BOMBE-SHELL

Turing set about trying to make something more elegant in its order, more sophisticated in its design than the Polish *bomba* that would be able to match Enigma, pace for pace. The resulting 'bombe' (both Bs are sounded) was built to Turing's specifications by Harold 'Doc' Keen (1894–1973). Chief engineer of British Tabulating Machines (BTM), a company that specialized in making time-punch clocks for workers in industry and commerce, Keen had the skills and experience needed to endow Turing's musings with electromechanical reality.

Rejewski's team had come up with the idea of the 'grill' – a way of trying out possible permutations of Enigma coding and narrowing down the available options by ruling out those correspondences that didn't seem to signify. Cryptographer Henryk Zygalski (1908–78) came up with the idea of using sheets of stiff paper, perforated in pre-set patterns, and named in his honour as 'Zygalski sheets'. Fed manually through the machine in succession, these progressively eliminated the impossible combinations, leaving a much smaller field of possibilities to be explored.

THE HUMAN FACTOR

Turing's response to the same challenge was not just brilliant but revealingly intuitive, anticipating the enormous importance he was ultimately to have in computer science. He didn't just rely on mathematical but on a more human logic – in its way, it took a step back to old-fashioned hand-ciphering. Turing incorporated the assumption that certain predictable forms of words were likely to be present in the Bombe's programming; conventional openings, for examples, or sign-off phrases. Once forms like these were identified, the codebreaker could work outward,

Below: The Bombe was intimidating alike in size, complexity and meticulous construction – but had it taken electromechanical engineering as far as it could go?

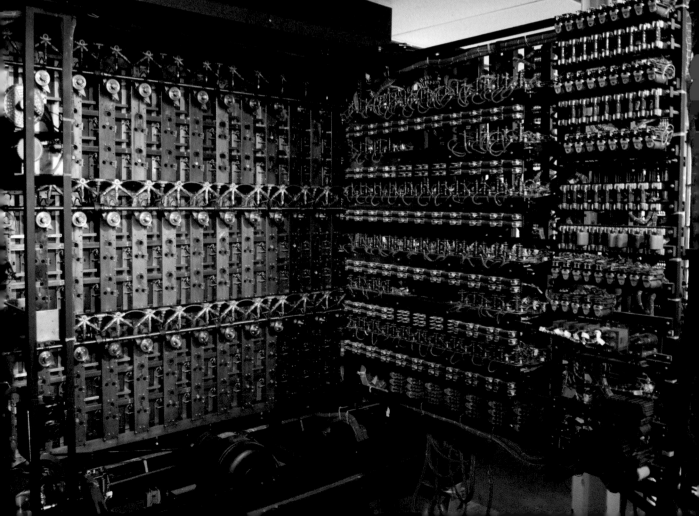

using the Bombe to run through the (now much narrower) field of available permutations.

The more conservative-minded might see this as evidence that Turing had identified important limitations of modern information technology right at the beginning of its history. Another way of looking at it is to see his approach as buttressing his claim to be the 'father' of an IT revolution that at its most forward-looking has always striven for the best possible 'fit' with the workings of the human mind.

As Gordon Welchman was to recognize, for instance, while use of the plugboard massively increased the range of possible substitutions open to the German cryptographers, it imported rigidities – and with them vulnerabilities – into their coding system. In substituting one letter for another, the system opened up 25 new possibilities to confuse the codebreaker. But it introduced one certainty: no letter could be itself. A fixed quantity like this is something the cryptanalyst can build on. Welchman was able to use it as a point of application. The 'diagonal board' he devised gave Turing's Bombe an additional dimension, allowing it to take advantage of this little glitch in Enigma's design.

It has been suggested that, had Axis cryptographers kept to their proper disciplines, no amount of British inspiration would have cracked their codes. The practical know-how assembled at Bletchley Park notwithstanding, workers were always wrestling what arguably were impossible odds. Sloppy procedures, repeated wordings, lazy formulations, unpoliced idiosyncrasies of style – these gave Bletchley Park a purchase, a way in. That said, the communications they read were themselves produced under real-world conditions by harassed, overworked and over-pressured cryptographers. It makes no sense to castigate them – or belittle Bletchley Park's achievement – on that basis. Neither

Alan Turing 1912–1954
Mathematician and WWII code breaker

Above: Movers, shakers, history makers. The Bombe shares the stage with Her Majesty the Queen on this commemorative stamp issued in 2012.

Above: These scrawlings by Alan Turing sold for over $1m. The holy relic of a secular saint? He certainly worked miracles.

should the power of the British codebreakers be overestimated – at least in these, the relatively early stages of their work. Miracles may have been worked, codes cracked and secret messages revealed, but the vast bulk of German communications were still getting through untouched.

A DISAPPOINTING START

Bletchley Park lacked the code-crunching capacity to deal with the volume of material already being intercepted. It followed that even when messages had been successfully decrypted, they came for the most part short of wider context. This meant they were still cryptic even when their wording was clear. This left officials higher up the intelligence hierarchy struggling to match the messages to existing situations on the ground.

Nor did adequate systems exist for information secured at Bletchley to be distributed quickly and securely. The bureaucracy was not geared up to make use of material coming from this new and unaccustomed source. These shortcomings were to be underlined emphatically in some of the first major fighting of the war. The Germans' invasion of neutral Norway in April 1940 was accompanied by a veritable blitz of signals traffic, an impressive amount of which was intercepted – and even successfully decoded. But what should have been an intelligence triumph fell flat: for want of a way of handling this harvest, most of it never made it beyond the walls of Bletchley Park; the material that did go up the line was too piecemeal and too late.

A LOST CAUSE?

A story can be 'mythic' and true at the same time. That of Bletchley Park is the perfect case. It's not that it didn't happen, or even that it didn't happen much as we've been told. What makes it mythic is the hold it has over our collective imaginations; the place it has taken in the way we think. The 'heroic' version of the story – of great brains computing and cogitating their way to victory – has become so important to our sense of how the world should work in this Information Age that we don't want to think

NORWAY NONSENSE

EXAMPLES OF BRITISH FAILURES in the first months of the war are not in short supply, but most have been overshadowed by Dunkirk. The encirclement of Britain's Expeditionary Force in France at the end of May 1940 represented (in Winston Churchill's words) a 'colossal military disaster'. That the episode came so quickly to be seen positively, in the light of the force's evacuation by an impromptu fleet of 'little ships', may be seen as a triumph of what would subsequently be called 'spin'.

Dunkirk distracted attention from other shortcomings in strategic planning at this time. The ease with which, from 9 April, German forces had overrun Denmark and Norway in Operation Weserübung would in any other circumstances have been seen as shocking. Norway's neutrality had never been taken seriously: neither side had any intention of respecting the integrity of a country whose port of Narvik commanded so crucial a corridor for Swedish iron ore.

Despite this, Britain's planning had been shambolic and its execution worse. The Royal Navy had been sent to mine Norwegian waters precisely to provoke

Above: Captured British and French soldiers are led away by German troops at Dunkirk.

a German attack. Then, when this had come, no real response had been prepared. As the intelligence community had already found, being ready for war in theory was not the same as being ready for the fight in practice.

about the more down-to-earth problems the project wrestled with. And, for longer than we care to remember, they wrestled with them unavailingly.

To this extent, the story meshes well with that of another English myth: that of the academy as an 'ivory tower', out of touch with the realities of the world. Historically, British popular opinion has been as quick to dismiss 'Oxbridge' as a place of self-involved ineffectiveness as it has to revere it for its intellectual endeavour. Even its friends could offer only double-edged praise: the poet (and 'Balliol Man') Matthew Arnold (1822–88) described his alma mater as the city of 'dreaming spires' – which hardly underlines its active contemporary relevance, any more than his other famous description of Oxford as 'home of lost causes, and forsaken beliefs'.

Oxbridge was, in other words, where superannuated thoughts and theories came to die: the idea that it might take Britain

FOR LIFE AND LINGERIE

'You walk and move with grace and poise. Why? Because you are giving *natural support* to tired and sagging muscles. That's what an individually designed Spirella can do for you.'

If the publicity for Spirella Corsetières was to be believed, their undergarments were a match in engineering sophistication for anything produced at Bletchley Park.

BTM's headquarters since 1920, Letchworth, Hertfordshire, lay just over 50km (33 miles) from Bletchley to the east, and only slightly further from central London to the south. The American firm Spirella had been the town's earliest major employer, establishing its British operation here in 1912.

Once the war began, Spirella's workers, overwhelmingly women, were asked to apply their skills to making parachutes. Soon, however – under conditions of the utmost secrecy – they were reassigned again, working at their benches in the Spirella Building but for BTM. Now they were no longer working with silk but with metal, making electromechanical components for assembly by BTM's technicians and for use by the codebreakers at Bletchley Park. Those delicate and dextrous fingers, trained to realize the 'exclusive design principle' that informed the Spirella corset, proved ideally suited to creating high-precision parts for Turing's Bombe.

INDIVIDUAL CORSETRY SERVICE

No two figures are alike. The Spirella method of INDIVIDUAL Corsetry recognises this—and caters accordingly.

At present limited to Surgical Service, as soon as restrictions are gone, we shall meet the needs of our pre-war clientele.

The
SPIRELLA COMPANY OF GREAT BRITAIN LIMITED
LETCHWORTH, HERTS,
and **SPIRELLA HOUSE, OXFORD CIRCUS, LONDON, W. 1**

forward could seem fanciful. As brilliant as the Bletchley Park achievement may have been in the abstract, the early evidence was that it wasn't going to make much difference.

It might easily have remained that way. That it didn't arguably owed less to Turing & Co, and the whole heroic narrative, than it did to more mundane decision-making. Bletchley Park might have stayed an ivory tower in the midst of a world at war if the authorities hadn't seen (albeit belatedly) the need to support their work. That meant, first, internal communications that could handle and distribute Ultra intelligence to those best qualified to interpret and to act upon it; second, a codebreaking operation adequate to the scale of the task it faced. The war years were to see a progressive industrialization of work at Bletchley Park: more, bigger Bombes, and more, better-trained codebreakers to work them.

Above: Their 'pre-war clientele' were going to have to wait: Spirella's workers would be unrecognised heroines in the building of the Bombe at Bletchley Park.

2

BLETCHLEY BEATS THE ITALIAN NAVY

A simple five-word message, deciphered by a teenage girl at Bletchley, gave Britain what Winston Churchill would acclaim as its greatest naval triumph since Trafalgar.

WAR? WHAT WAR? The Egyptian coast was quiet and calm; Alexandria was ablaze with spring sunshine; the sea was sparkling like a jewel, and it was just the afternoon for a round of golf. Admiral Andrew Cunningham (1883–1963) might have been in command of the Royal Navy's fleet in the Mediterranean, but he had more pressing duties on his mind right now. The afternoon of 27 March 1941 saw him arriving at his country club, armed with his overnight case and his bag of clubs. He was ready for anything the eighteen holes had to throw at him; firm in his resolve to follow his five-iron to death or glory. Dirty work, but someone had to do it. His game over, he'd adjourn to the clubhouse, change for a dinner party in the city, where – rather than making the return trip to his flagship, HMS *Warspite* – he'd stay the night. He'd done this many times since he'd been posted here. He was an Englishman abroad, yet completely and utterly at his ease.

Opposite: The fire of blazing warships lights up the sky off Greece's Cape Matapan, a catastrophic defeat for Italy's *Regia Marina*.

Not that he was the only one keeping calm and golfing on: foreign businessmen, officials, diplomats … all ex-pat Alexandria was here. So exclusive was this club, so far removed did it feel from the war, that its membership cut across the customary Allied–Axis lines. That very afternoon, Cunningham coincided with the Japanese Consul at the club, but no one gave their near-meeting a moment's thought. The Admiral only raised his voice while he continued his conversation with a colleague about the party that was in prospect for that evening.

A little later, he slipped out unnoticed and headed back to his ship. The much-discussed dinner party didn't happen. Instead, quietly and quickly, preparations were made for the *Warspite*'s departure, and by 1900 hours that evening she was leaving port.

Below: Admiral Andrew Cunningham's tactical nous and seamanship were even better than his golf game, winning him one of the Royal Navy's greatest triumphs.

POINTS OF VIEW

If, in the annals of warfare, the story of the admiral's interrupted shore leave doesn't resonate, this was the intention all along. World War II may have brought us *blitzkrieg*, Operation Barbarossa, the attack on Pearl Harbor, the bombing of Dresden, the Tokyo Firestorm and other spectacular shows of force, but it was also in important ways a war of stealth. Was it in *more* important ways a war of stealth? How do we begin to address that question? How do we hope to compare the contribution of Bletchley Park with those of the men who made the Normandy Landings or attacked Berlin? Much depends on perspective. Dilly Knox, notoriously, used to ask new recruits which way the hands of a clock went round. 'From left to right,' came the answer, invariably. That was why it was called 'clockwise'. As their commander immediately reminded them, though, it depended on which way you were facing: from the clock's point of view, the hands revolved in the opposite direction.

This was an important point, and vital for a would-be codebreaker to take on board, given his or her need to get inside the enemy's consciousness. It is essential for us too if we are to get a clear sense both of the nature of the work the Bletchley Park codebreakers carried out and the comparative importance of its contribution overall.

GUESSING GAMES
The story behind the Admiral's country club visit begins in Bletchley a few days earlier, on 25 March, where a vital

Below: Punch Room, C Block, Bletchley. Victory at Cape Matapan was won by the men at sea, but they couldn't have done it without 'Dilly and his girls', Cunningham confessed.

HMS *WARSPITE*

No ship is ever just a steel and wood construction, given the human stories surrounding it; still less any naval vessel, given the history it accrues. Least of all, perhaps, any ship bearing the name *Warspite* – which has been in almost continuous use since the sixteenth century. In that time, it's been borne by no fewer than seven vessels: the first one went with Sir Walter Raleigh (c. 1554–1618) to Cádiz. Successors fought in the Anglo-Dutch Wars of the seventeenth century and the Napoleonic Wars in the nineteenth. Cunningham's ship was a veteran of Jutland (1916). However charismatic the name, its origin remains obscure: the word 'warspite' was popularly used for the woodpecker, and the first few *Warspites* were to damage their fair share of timber. But it may just represent the bitter 'spite' of battle.

breakthrough had been made. As befits the looking-glass world we find ourselves in whenever we try to comprehend the Bletchley Park achievement, the drama of the situation seemed in inverse proportion to its importance. It all came down to a guessing game.

Dilly Knox had already shown the importance to the codebreaker of being able to intuit the sort of mental and cultural structures upon which the cryptographer might be building. Anything he or she could do to find patterns or predictability in the codes they were wrestling with improved the chances of those codes being cracked. At Bletchley Park, he encouraged his younger staff to attempt the same sort of intuitive leaps in tackling the intercepted Italian intelligence messages they had been receiving – all enciphered in Enigma code.

LEVERAGE

DILLY'S STAR ASSISTANT (AND, many years later, his biographer) Mavis Lever is now generally known as Mavis Batey (1921–2013), following her marriage in 1942 to her Bletchley Park colleague, Keith Batey (1919–2010). A Carlisle-born and Cambridge-educated mathematician, Keith was a figure right off Gordon Welchman's provincial production line. Mavis was a South Londoner and the daughter of a seamstress and a postman. She may have had more in common with Keith than with many of the often posher 'Bletchley Girls'.

Despite her humble origins, Mavis was highly educated, having won a place at Coloma Convent, outside Croydon – a free but academically selective grammar school. From there, she'd won a place at University College, London (UCL), to study German, which aroused official interest when the hostilities began. Before being sent to Bletchley, she was based in London, where she searched personal ads in the *Times* in hopes of finding coded messages for German spies.

'Organization is not a word you would associate with Dilly Knox,' she recalled years later, and he didn't believe in elaborate inductions. 'I was never really told what to do,' she said. But, she concluded, 'I think … that was a great precedent in my life, because he taught me to think that you could do things yourself without always checking up to see what the book said.'

Whatever her initial hesitations, Mavis quickly made herself one of Bletchley Park's most self-confidently intuitive and creative codebreakers.

Mavis Lever proved particularly adept, making up in intuition what she lacked in experience. Just nineteen, she had interrupted her German studies at London University to join the staff at Bletchley Park a year before. Working with Knox on cracking the Italian Naval Code, she had for some time been trying out likely forms of words to see if she could identify set formulae across multiple messages and find more exact letter equivalences that way. One surmise that yielded important progress was that one cryptographer had a girlfriend, Rosa, and habitually used her name in making up his codes.

Another guess had taken Levis (via the suspicion that one recurrent opener might mean 'Per', for 'Personale' and a series of consequent deductions) to a sound-seeming interpretation of the then-current Italian code. Based on what she'd learned, she'd been able to build up a more comprehensive picture. Soon she and her colleagues were routinely reading the Italian messages.

Above: Like many other women, Mavis Lever (later Batey) was to find a new sense of self-confidence through her wartime work at Bletchley Park.

GUESS AGAIN

The guesswork was just beginning, though, for even when a message had been decrypted, the operational context that gave it real meaning wasn't known. So when Mavis Lever worked out that one five-word phrase could be translated as "Today 25 March is X-3", no one was any the wiser as to what was meant.

However, higher-ups in London and commanders on the ground (or, in this case, at sea) were able to read Mavis' message alongside other information they'd been receiving over a period of days and even weeks. These had already alerted them to the fact that Axis naval forces had something planned for the eastern Mediterranean. That the translated message had been sent from

A TALE OF TWO TRAWLERS

ON 30 APRIL 1940, while the battle for Norway was still going on, HMS *Griffin* had been patrolling off the coast. There it had stumbled upon the *Polares*, by its flag and description a Dutch trawler, but actually a well-armed German vessel in disguise. As a party from the British destroyer went aboard, a crewman was seen tossing two large bags into the sea. One floated long enough to be recovered. It was taken, with the *Polares*, back to Orkney's Scapa Flow.

Inside were confidential documents, including pads containing 'keys' comparing plain and cipher text. Although these papers provided the codes for only five days' signalling, others included hints as to how the regular codes were likely to be modified. They were only hints, though, and only likely to be accessible through long, arduous and repetitive trial and error. For meaningful access, further information would be needed.

Above: Sunken ships left a scene of devastation in Narvik fjord in April 1940.

Above: A box of Enigma wheels was found aboard the *Krebs*.

That came the following March when British Commandos attacking the northerly Lofoten Islands captured another armed trawler, the *Krebs*. Not only did they find a full month's worth of naval codes but also a complete set of Enigma rotor-wheels. Even now, no all-revealing 'key' had been discovered. Bletchley Park's codebreakers still had a great deal to do. But the challenge they faced had slipped from being all but insurmountable to merely extremely difficult. And that was the kind of challenge they felt up to.

Rome to the Italian Commander in Rhodes suggested some connection with this venture – perhaps a landing in Libya, London mused.

Other information made this seem less likely, though. Orders were given for German fighter planes in Libya to be moved to Sicily, while the Italians were asked to bomb the airport in British-held Crete. When a further message made clear that a battle group was about to set out from Italy headed for the Aegean, the likelihood seemed that they were being sent to attack troopships carrying British soldiers as part of Operation Lustre. Crete lay about midway between Alexandria and Athens and was an important base for Allied aircraft in the region.

AS A PARTY FROM THE BRITISH DESTROYER WENT ABOARD, A CREWMAN WAS SEEN TOSSING TWO LARGE BAGS INTO THE SEA. ONE FLOATED LONG ENOUGH TO BE RECOVERED.

READY AND WAITING

Whatever the Italians were up to, it couldn't hurt to intervene – and thanks to Bletchley Park, the opportunity was there to catch them napping; hence the subterfuge around the party on the *Warspite* and Admiral Cunningham's escapade ashore. It was assumed that the Japanese Consul would report having seen the Admiral on the golf course and overhearing his conversation

Below: The Savoia Marchetti SM 79 Sparviero ('Sparrowhawk') bomber/torpedo plane had been playing havoc with British shipping in the Mediterranean.

about the evening's dinner party; consequently it would be assumed that he and his flagship weren't going anywhere.

In the early hours of 27 March, accordingly, when an Italian fleet put out from Naples and set a course southeast towards the Aegean, its commander could apparently assume that they were doing so undetected. Squadron Vice-Admiral Angelo Iachino (1889–1976) must have been feeling pretty confident, with only a few troopships and their token escorts to contend with. Not that he'd necessarily have felt vulnerable in any case. Built just four years previously, in 1937, his flagship, the battleship *Vittorio Veneto*, was a veritable floating fortress, displacing some 45,000 tons and armed with nine 380-mm (15-inch) guns. With her was an escort of destroyers.

A trio of heavy (that is, 10,000-ton) cruisers – the *Zara, Fiume and Pola* – was to rendezvous with the *Vittorio Veneto* group in the Strait of Messina, between the Italian mainland and Sicily. Admiral Luigi Sansonetti (1888–1950) had command

OPERATION LUSTRE

ALTHOUGH SLOW IN GETTING off the mark, the building of Mussolini's New Roman Empire had slowly gained momentum as territories first in Africa and then southeastern Europe had been taken. Albania had been occupied in April 1939; in October 1940, Italian forces had invaded Greece. By the turn of the year, however, it was becoming clear that they were running into difficulties. The Greeks were fighting back fiercely, and with some success. As the weeks went by, it came to seem inevitable that Germany would have to come to its Axis ally's rescue and launch its own invasion from the north.

Although by no means a military or economic superpower, Greece remained important to the Allies, partly as a base for air attacks on the Romanian oilfields that were strategically vital to the Germans. It was also significant symbolically: with so much of western Europe already occupied, it seemed crucial that some precedent be set for the German juggernaut being stopped; hence the decision to mount Operation Lustre. Throughout March 1941, convoys left Alexandria for Athens. Some 60,000 troops, with tanks and artillery, were shipped from Egypt (where they'd been protecting Suez) to assist in the defence of Greece. The ultimately unavailing defence of Greece, however: this force had to be evacuated again at the end of April.

of this group. Three further heavy cruisers – the *Trieste*, *Trento* and *Bolzano* – were going to join them from Taranto under the command of Admiral Carlo Cattaneo (1883–1941). This group was attended by four destroyers: the *Vittorio Alfieri*, the *Giosuè Carducci*, the *Vincenzo Gioberti* and the *Alfredo Oriani*. A couple of light cruisers (the *Duca degli Abruzzo* and *Giuseppe Garibaldi*) came from Brindisi. Altogether, this was a formidable fighting group. Their orders were to muster off the island of Gavdo, south of Crete, then push north and east around Crete itself into the Aegean, attacking Allied shipping as they went.

In fact, Iachino was to find himself outnumbered and outgunned: Cunningham's *Warspite*, weighing in at 33,000 tons, might have been a veteran of *Jutland* (1916), but she'd been completely rebuilt and massively modernized since then: in essentials, she was as up-to-date as the *Vittorio Veneto*. And the *Warspite* was only one of three battleships in the group setting off from Alexandria; HMS *Barham* and *Valiant* were there as well. So too, along with the aircraft carrier HMS *Formidable*, were two flotillas of destroyers: the 10th (HMS *Greyhound* and *Griffin* and an Australian ship, HMAS *Stuart*) and the 14th

Above: Commissioned in 1931, the *Fiume* was a casualty of Cape Matapan, one of five ships sunk on a disastrous day for the Italian navy.

(HMS *Jervis*, *Janus*, *Mohawk* and *Nubian*), along with a couple more destroyers, HMS *Havock* and *Hotspur*.

Admiral Sir Henry Pridham-Wippell (1885–1952), master of HMS *Ajax*, was in command of a second force, setting out at the same time from Piraeus in the south of Greece. This force included light cruisers such as the *Ajax* and HMS *Orion* and *Gloucester* and Australia's HMAS *Perth*, as well as destroyers HMS *Hasty*, *Ilex* and *Hereward*. Other Allied ships were waiting in the wings, some engaged in escorting the Alexandria convoys, but already discreetly apprised of Italian intentions; more were loitering in the waters off northern Crete.

THE ELEMENT OF SURPRISE

As the opposing fleets converged, one commander believed he had the advantage of surprise and was keen to keep it; the other actually *did* have that advantage, but was at pains to lose it. Although he'd taken such care to cover up his embarkation

Below: The heavy cruiser *Bolzano* comes under attack at Cape Matapan. In the event she was able to escape more or less unscathed.

and departure, now that battle was imminent Cunningham's main concern was to let Iachino know he knew that he was coming. This was not easy, given the other great weakness of the Italian fleet: not even the *Vittorio Veneto* was equipped with radar.

As empowering as ULTRA intelligence might be, it always came with an accompanying headache: what if its application tipped off the enemy to its existence? If the Allies had the jump on the Germans or Italians, how were they supposed to have got it? How many times could such successes convincingly be attributed to luck? However tempting a triumph might be, Britain could not afford to rush in regardless and risk the Axis catching on that its codes were being broken and its signals read.

A commander, said Prussian military theorist Carl von Clausewitz (1780–1831), only gets one complete surprise – once he's had it, that's his big advantage gone. As the war went on, the Allies found themselves facing sometimes agonizing dilemmas as to how far and how openly they dared to play their hand.

For now, it was straightforward enough for a Sunderland flying boat to be sent up from Crete and – apparently by chance, during a routine patrol – sight Iachino's flotilla sailing southward. It was, of course, more important that the Italians should sight the Sunderland 'sighting' them – that would explain the Allies' awareness of what was happening. This was not just for the Italians' benefit: the *Warspite*'s officers and crew were also told that the *Vittorio Veneto* group had been discovered by 'reconnaissance': ULTRA's secrecy had to be protected at all costs.

Above: Angelo Iachino was the first of a succession of talented, experienced and committed commanders to be bested (without ever knowing it) by Bletchley Park.

CHANGE OF PLAN

The tactic worked almost too well. Iachino was worried enough to report to his headquarters that his flotilla had been seen. His superiors at the *Supermarina* in Rome were still more perturbed, having received separate intelligence that the carrier

Above: The carrier HMS *Formidable* was built in 1940. The ship's aircraft were to play a vital role at Cape Matapan.

a shipmate on that vessel's bridge between bites of a sandwich. 'I thought ours were miles away.' As indeed they were, leaving Pridham-Wippell's cruisers dangerously exposed when Iachino's flagship opened fire: more than twenty salvos, amounting to more than 90 shells.

Despite their earlier difficulties, the Italian gunners found the right range with speed this time, and several of their shells missed the *Orion* by only yards. But a succession of jams brought a hiatus in the hail of gunfire, giving Pridham-Wippell's force a few vital minutes to get away. By the time the *Vittorio Veneto* was opening up again, the British ships were far enough away to feel more secure.

A FORMIDABLE THREAT

By now, the afternoon wearing on, Admiral Cunningham and his Alexandria contingent were approaching. They were still more than 110km (60 miles) away, though, and moving comparatively slowly. Cunningham realized he'd have to play for time. As far away as it was, the Italian fleet was within the range of Fairey Albacores from HMS *Formidable*. They would take up the strain, the admiral decided.

A little anachronistic-looking now, as biplanes, the Albacores were nevertheless faster than the Fairey Swordfish they were gradually replacing. They weren't quite as manoeuvrable, though, and their pilots were still to be convinced that they really represented an improvement. Even so, these three-man planes were widely used in naval reconnaissance as well as bombing. (The Fairey Swordfish was still serving – and with distinction: several were to be involved in the Battle of Cape Matapan.)

The Albacores were deployed as torpedo bombers in this engagement. Although a first wave was fended off by anti-aircraft fire from the Italian ships, a second managed to get closer. One plane was within a mile of the *Vittorio Veneto* when it loosed a torpedo that, right on target, holed the hull, damaged a propellor and brought the battleship to a halt.

The news, Cunningham reported, sent 'a thrill of elation' through his fleet. This was premature, however. A sophisticated system of watertight compartments contained the damage to the battleship. A few hours later, after some frantic pumping and hasty repair work, the *Vittorio Veneto* was on the move again. More slowly, though, so as evening approached Cunningham had a further wave of Albacores and Swordfish sent after the Italian flagship to follow through. They were joined by land-based bombers sent from Crete.

Below: The *Vittorio Veneto* might have held her own against the Royal Navy – but could hardly contend with the Navy and Bletchley Park.

Iachino was ready for them. A series of salvos, along with smokescreens and searchlights from the *Vittorio Veneto* and its escorting vessels, dazzled and confused the crews of the attacking planes; some cleverly choreographed zigzags threw them further and the Italians successfully kept their flagship safe. In the chaos, though, the *Pola* had nearly rammed the *Fiume*. A sitting target for a torpedo-bomber, it was duly hit – caught square, amidships on the starboard side. Five boilers were destroyed and the main steamline severed by the explosion; that meant a total electrical failure, the shutdown of the engines, and one heavy cruiser left floating helplessly.

Despite the damage done by carrier-based aircraft, Iachino did not appreciate how close the *Formidable* was by now, or how hard Cunningham's fleet was pressing at his heels. Although he received information from the *Supermarina* that there were British ships in his vicinity, he took this to mean Pridham-Wippell's smaller and comparatively unintimidating force. 'I had not the slightest idea that we were being pursued so closely by the British fleet,' he later recalled. Had he known, he said, 'I should have abandoned the *Pola* to her fate.'

Instead, he sent several ships back to go to the *Pola*'s aid. These included her sister-cruisers the *Zara* and the *Fiume* and three destroyers. Evening fell with the *Fiume* riding at close quarters by the *Pola*'s bow, its crew struggling to get a towline to the stricken cruiser.

NIGHT WATCH

Darkness fell, with the *Pola* adrift and her would-be rescuers clustering around her, and with the balance of strength between the two opposing forces abruptly skewed. For the British vessels, with their radar, the coming of darkness made little difference, but the Italians, to all intents and purposes, were blind.

Radar ('Radio Direction and Ranging') had been developed in fits and starts through the 1930s in the United States and Britain (other countries – including Germany – had been working on their own versions). It was still a new technology and less than perfect, despite having played a vital role for the RAF in the

Opposite: The *Formidable*'s Fairey Albacores were to inflict serious damage on the Italian fleet. Here, however, wings folded, they seem peaceful enough.

Above: Italy's destroyers, a potent threat, were compromised at Cape Matapan not just by ULTRA intelligence but by their lack of radar.

Battle of Britain the year before. But it basically allowed those British ships that were equipped with it to 'see' the Italian vessels while remaining concealed. HMS *Warspite*, with the *Valiant* and the *Barham*, was able to creep up on the oblivious Italians, approaching to a distance of around 3.5km (2 miles).

On Cunningham's command, his men threw the switches on their searchlights: the enemy ships stood out as clear as day and the Royal Navy gunners were able to fire at will. Their opposite numbers, meanwhile, milled about, completely unprepared for a night attack like this one. Five 860kg (1938lb) shells smacked straight into the *Fiume* – one of its turrets was completely blown away. And that was just the first salvo; rocked by blast after blast, the cruiser was soon aflame from stem to stern.

'A TERRIFIC BURST'

The ambush having been successfully sprung, the remaining British ships joined in the attack. Watching from HMAS *Stuart* was Chief Signals Yeoman Watkins: 'The sky opened up ... at least it seemed so,' he remembered later:

A moment after the Warspite *fired the leading cruiser burst into a mass of flames right from one end of the ship to the other.*

Then the second cruiser burst into flames as a salvo from either the Barham *or* Valiant *caught her. By this time, a matter of seconds after the first gun, the air was full of noise, searchlights, tracers and spray. The* Greyhound *and* Griffin*...had opened upon the destroyers.*

Star shell were hovering in the sky and the tracers from Breda bullets twined a vivid line across the dark background.

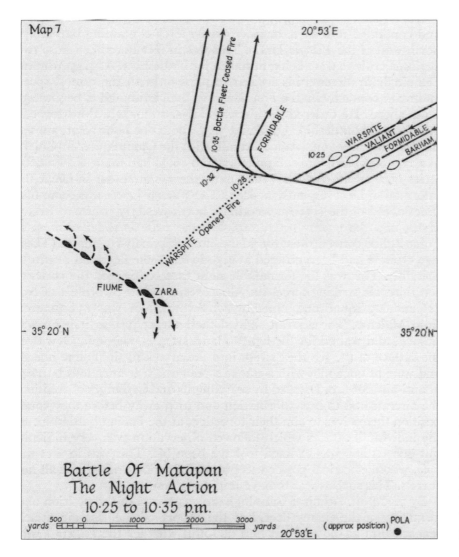

Map 7

20°53'E

10·35 Battle Fleet Ceased Fire

FORMIDABLE

10·25

WARSPITE
VALIANT
FORMIDABLE
BARHAM

10·32

10·28

WARSPITE 'Opened Fire'

FIUME   ZARA

35°20'N

35°20'N

Battle Of Matapan
The Night Action
10·25 to 10·35 p.m.

500   0   1000   2000   3000
yards   yards   20°53'E

(approx position) POLA

Left: Their possession of radar – and the enemy's lack of it – allowed HMS *Warspite* to stalk the *Fiume* and *Zara* at laughably close quarters.

HMS *Havock* hit an Italian destroyer:

It was a terrific burst. The magazine must have been hit, for a billow of flames shot up and from inside this rose a further mushroom head of flame of even greater brilliancy. As suddenly as it rose, it vanished, leaving dense smoke.

The *Fiume* was rapidly sinking. Sansonetti could only look on helplessly as the *Vittorio Alfieri* went up in 'an enormous flame'. *Suddenly I heard the sound of explosions. I ran out and saw large pieces flying through the air.*

Isolated now, her sister-destroyer the *Giosuè Carducci* could be used for target practice by the Allied gunners. She was all but obliterated by a succession of heavy shells. The *Zara*, meanwhile, was adrift, crippled and defenceless – she was finished off by a torpedo a while later.

Long gone by now, Iachino and the *Vittorio Veneto* waited for further orders but, not receiving any, pushed homeward as

Below: The *Valiant* (foreground), *Barham* and *Warspite* crept up under the cover of darkness and bombarded the *Zara* and *Fiume* from point-blank range.

fast as they could. A determined pursuit might have caught them, Cunningham knew. But it would also bring her hunters within range of land-based Axis aircraft – and that might produce an ugly outcome.

Above: A British ship picks up survivors in the aftermath of the battle. In the region of a thousand were to be saved.

KEEPING SCORE

By the time the sun came up and the smoke had cleared, 2400 Italian lives had been lost. So too – and, in the cold accountancy of war, more importantly – had five ships, not to mention the pride of Italy's navy, the *Regia Marina*. Efforts by Cunningham's crews to rescue survivors were thwarted by attacking German aircraft, it being deemed (and again, in these inhuman circumstances, the calculation would have been quite rational) that a large group of Allied vessels hove-to in the mid-Mediterranean was too tempting a target to miss.

Even so, around a thousand survivors were saved, all Italian. The British had lost only three lives when the crew of a torpedo-bomber was shot down. None of Cunningham's ships had been significantly damaged.

ITALIAN NAVY BATTERED

BATTLESHIP AND TWO CRUISERS DAMAGED

ONE CERTAINLY SUNK

MEN FOR WAR WORK

REGISTRATION ON SATURDAY

EXEMPTED TRADES

NEAR EAST IS LINING UP

YUGOSLAVIA AS BULWARK

THE EFFECT ON HUNGARY

NAZIS THREATEN YUGOSLAVIA

ACTION IF "ORDER" IS NOT RESTORED

STATE OF SIEGE IN COUNTRY

THE BATTLE OF BRITAIN

STAYING POWER OF THE R.A.F.

HOW GERMANY FAILED

"ACHTUNG, SCHPITFEUER!"

Above: London's *Observer* makes the most of the Cape Matapan victory – as bracing for British morale as it was devastating for Italian.

Comparisons with Trafalgar were hyperbolic, maybe. But how is the importance of any battle to be judged? It is not just a philosophical question. If Churchill was talking up his Navy's triumph for the sake of boosting to general military (and national) morale, that tactic clearly made sense at the time. A bit of good news from Greece was overdue.

The news was certainly welcome at Bletchley Park when it came by a phone call the following night from Naval Intelligence Director John Godfrey (1888–1970). In Dilly's absence, his assistant Edward Clarke received the Government's congratulations. 'Tell Dilly that we have won a great victory in the Mediterranean,' Godfrey said, 'and it is entirely due to him and his girls.' A few weeks later, Admiral Cunningham turned up in person to thank the codebreakers for their efforts.

This was a nice fillip – but, like the victory itself, much more than that in its implications for staff morale. The admiral's visit was unprecedented – as, indeed, Godfrey's praise had been. And, given justifiable security concerns, there would not be much more feedback of this kind. Work at Bletchley Park might be physically safe, but it was boring and abstract. If there were intellectual satisfactions, it never felt much like fighting a war. The news from Cape Matapan brought home to Bletchley staff the real-world relevance and significance of their daily work; the impact it could have for those fighting the war at first hand, by land, air and sea.

SURREALITIES AT SEA

It is difficult to see past the spin to the real history behind it, but just how historic was the Battle of Cape Matapan? If it was so important, why have only aficionados of naval history heard of it nowadays? Might it be important *because* most of us haven't heard of it? In the modern mythohistory of World War

SEDUCED BY CYNTHIA?

Above: The 'Cynthia' story was as seductive as the woman herself could ever have been.

THE ROUT OF THE *Regia Marina* at Cape Matapan inevitably sparked much speculation. How had Iachino's fleet been caught out so badly? Could it really have been by luck that the flying boat had come across the most important expedition the

Italians had mounted for some time? With national pride at stake, rumours continued about the possible role of an Allied spy. And who better to act as focus for such stories than Amy Elizabeth Thorpe (1910–63). The Minneapolis-born daughter of a senior US Marines officer and his wife, a state senator's daughter, Miss Thorpe grew up with a love of adventure and intrigue. Brought up in Washington D.C., she'd had a succession of affairs with foreign diplomats by the time she was twenty. In World War II, as 'Cynthia', she had affairs with Axis diplomats – and reported their secrets to US Intelligence.

One alleged object of her affections was the Italian Naval Attaché, Admiral Alberto Lais (1882–1951), who, it is suggested, revealed important operational details to her. When the English author Harford Montgomery Hyde (1907–89) claimed as much in a biography of 'Cynthia' in the 1960s, however, Lais' family angrily sued. In truth, regardless of the content of the Attaché's pillow talk, Bletchley Park and ULTRA had given the Allies what they needed.

II, that the Italian contribution to the Axis effort is regarded with some amusement may owe as much to north European and Anglo-Saxon condescension as to fact. But this body blow to the *Regia Marina* at such a comparatively early point in the conflict helps explain what amounts to its virtual disappearance from the narrative from this time on. Mavis Lever would recall that this was 'practically the last we would hear of the Italian

SHARING WITH STALIN

IF BRITAIN FELT IT could barely trust its own commanders with ULTRA intelligence, how was it to feel comfortable sharing it with the Soviet Union? How, for that matter, was Josef Stalin (1878–1953) to feel comfortable receiving information from such a source? Churchill's record of resistance to Nazism might have been unimpeachable, but he was also a committed anti-Communist. After the October Revolution of 1917 he had been quick to urge that the Western allies should 'strangle the Bolshevik baby in its cradle'.

With Operation Barbarossa (1941), however, Russia's priorities abruptly rearranged themselves. Now an alliance with the West was necessary. It was the same for Britain, the United States and their Allies: little as they might like the idea of working with the Soviets, they were going to need them to do the heavy lifting.

Britain passed on its Bletchley Park intelligence where it seemed relevant to the Russians, but under the pretence of its being what we would now call HUMINT (human intelligence, secured by the work of old-fashioned human spies). The Russians weren't to know that the British had broken the German codes. Such was the cat's cradle of spying and counter-spying between East and West, however, that by 1942 Stalin was getting the inside story straight from Bletchley Park via his own human contact: John Cairncross (1913–95), who would not be unmasked until 1952.

By that time, it is thought, he'd passed on some 6000 documents – an enormous haul of information, by any standards. Quite how complete an inside story Cairncross was giving the Russians, though – quite how clear they were on where these secrets had originated or how they'd been secured – remains hotly disputed.

Stalin, for his part, won't have wanted to look the gift-horse too closely in the mouth. Key for him would have been that Cairncross's communications more or less matched those he got from Churchill. His first inclination had been to treat Britain's unwonted generosity with deep suspicion. Cairncross's contribution would have served as a sort of guarantee.

fleet, which only made one more appearance before surrendering to Cunningham in 1943'.

Thanks to Cunningham's victory here, a strong and potentially influential force was effectively removed from the military equation. Modest as he may have been about his own contribution, the Admiral had no doubt as to Cape Matapan's importance, both in the immediate term and more enduringly. 'There is little doubt,' he reflected later, 'that the rough handling given the enemy on this occasion served us in good stead during the evacuations of Greece and Crete. Much of these later operations may be said to have been conducted under the cover of the Battle of Matapan.'

Above: The highest self-sacrifice: Winston and Josef pose together, the picture of amity, putting mutual contempt aside for the greater good.

Iachino disagreed, but really only in his emphases. He didn't accept the British view that the *Regia Marina* had been demoralized. But his claim that the defeat had 'revealed our inferiority in effective aero-naval cooperation and the backwardness of our night battle technology' might be seen as amounting to the same thing.

Can we have a history of what hasn't happened? The codebreaking operation of Bletchley Park was based on this sort of second-guessing; this kind of upending of convention. Decryption depended on an ability to 'think backwards'. Why not a historiography of Conan Doyle's 'dog that didn't bark'? Of Dilly's clock's-eye view?

Above: Many important commanders were to see their reputations undone by ULTRA – some, like Sir Hugh Dowding, were on the Allied side.

the strength and disposition of forces arrayed against the Netherlands on the eve of their invasion, for instance. But the most detailed intelligence was no substitute for actual forces on the ground and in the air, and at this stage in the war the initiative was very much with the Germans.

(NOT QUITE) THEIR FINEST HOUR

So it continued into the summer of 1940. In theory, ULTRA information was available to the 'Few' defending England's southern coasts during the Battle of Britain. In practice, though, with German signals crews exchanging the rotors in their Enigma machines daily, British codebreakers were left floundering in their wake.

It wasn't just the decryption itself for which there was a steep and unforgiving learning curve: knowing how to use decrypted information – and when not to – remained a challenge. Head of the RAF, Air Chief Marshal Sir Hugh Dowding (1882–1970), had access to secret communications obtained by Bletchley Park, but couldn't tell his service colleagues. Inevitably, he had trouble communicating the need for actions that could, on the face of it, seem perverse – so much so that he was sacked in the days following his Battle of Britain victory. Without jeopardizing the security of the ULTRA secret, his superiors could not protect him. Unable to defend his direction of Fighter Command through the most crucial months of its existence, he had to fall on his sword for the greater good.

The general consensus after the Battle of Britain, and through much of the postwar period, was that radar had given the RAF its edge. Despite what we know of ULTRA now, that probably remains true: the amount of decrypted information available was so limited, and the restrictions on its use so stringent. Even so, with the balance of advantage in the fight for the skies so finely poised, every little must have helped.

FROM INVASION TO BLITZ

It was much the same with Operation Sea Lion, Hitler's plan
for an invasion of England across the Channel, intended to be
his climactic conclusion to the Battle of Britain. Many messages
were read, but mostly too late to assist the military planning.
Fortunately, the defeat of the *Luftwaffe* meant that the necessary
air cover would not be available, so invasion plans had to be
shelved. It was a coup for Bletchley Park, when, on 17 September
that year, staff decrypted instructions for paratroopers waiting
at a Belgian airfield to be stood down and moved out with their
equipment: implicit confirmation that Sea Lion was off.

Below: Invasion barges
crowd Boulogne harbour
in readiness for Operation
Sea Lion. Decrypted
messages helped British
commanders make
preparations for the
aborted invasion.

   Not that England was off
the hook. Defeat in the Battle of
Britain may have denied them
daytime superiority in the skies,
but the *Luftwaffe*'s bombers
were still able to come and
go at night. Not at will, and
certainly not without opposition
from the RAF's fighters and
from ground-based gunners,
but come and go they did, and
to devastating effect. While
ULTRA information tipped
off the authorities to German
plans for Operation Moonlight
Sonata (14 November 1940), the
assumption was that this massive
air raid was to be directed at
London, as so many others had
been. (Churchill even changed
his plans, returning to Downing
Street from the country so he
could be present in the capital.)
Instead, the Midlands city of
Coventry was severely damaged
and more than 500 people

Opposite: Claims that
codebreakers warned of
the Coventry blitz – but
that the authorities stayed
silent to keep the ULTRA
secret – have now been
generally discredited.

killed. Britain was finding that intelligence didn't just have to be
reliable; it had to come with sufficient context to be truly useful.

At the time, Operation Sea Lion's abandonment didn't feel so
complete a deliverance as might be imagined now. The Blitz on
Britain's cities was still going on – intensifying, even. In any case,
if the rest of Europe fell to Nazi control, Britain wouldn't be free
and sovereign in any meaningful sense. No one felt that more
strongly than Churchill. That said, the lifting of the immediate
invasion threat at least allowed him to think more strategically.

'LUCKY' IN LIBYA

This brings us to North Africa, where Britain had already taken
the initiative and Italian commander Rodolfo 'Lucky' Graziani
(1896–1940) was under mounting pressure from Mussolini to

BENDING THE BEAMS

IT WAS A LUCKY break for Bletchley Park
that the comparatively few coded messages
being readily decrypted at this time included
those being sent back and forth between
Germany's bombers and their bases. The
codebreakers classified these as 'Brown'
communications, and of course they yielded
life-saving information on where air raids
were most imminently to be expected.

Intriguingly, these messages included
navigational details – not only aircrafts'
precise position and directions, but where
they were in relation to the radio 'beams'
they were supposed to be following to
their targets. The Luftwaffe had come
up with a highly sophisticated response
to the challenge of night-navigation
for its bombers, triangulating beams of
radio waves from transmitters far apart
in mainland Europe. These beams were
directed so as to meet exactly above their
British target. When the plane's receiver
registered that meeting, the crew could drop
its bombs.

Workers at Bletchley discovered that, if
they were ingenious and quick enough, they
could make these beams work for them. As
Oliver Lawn (1919–) explained:

*There was a code, which set the angle
of the beams. And if you could break the
code, clever engineers could bend one of
the beams so that the crossing point was
over green fields, and not over cities.*

One raid, intended to devastate
Derby, an important industrial town (and
headquarters of Rolls Royce, supplier of
Spitfire engines, among many other things)
is known to have been averted in this way.

Above: Tracked vehicles like these British Vickers tanks came into their own in the North African desert – but brought tactical and logistical challenges with them.

take it back. His complaints that his forces were too poorly equipped and supplied to be capable of effective action were ignored by his leader back in Rome – just as Balbo's complaints before him had been.

A British presence in North Africa had been established in 1936, under the Anglo-Egyptian Treaty, which in return for protection for Egypt had allowed Britain control over the Suez Canal. British troops – along with men from India, Australia, New Zealand, Rhodesia and other Commonwealth countries – had been installed along the course of the Canal, and in some strength.

On 14 June, a small force from here had breached the Italian Frontier Wire, crossed into Libya and taken Fort Capuzzo, not far from Sallum. They didn't linger, but demolished fortifications and destroyed materiel. This was a small but significant step that cast a shadow over Italy's entrance into a war in which German forces seemed to be carrying all before them.

Two days later came more bad news: an attempted fightback had seen the Italians coming off soundly beaten in the war's first tank battle. En route to Fort Capuzzo, a squadron of tanks and armoured cars with infantry had been waylaid by the British at Nezuct Ghirba, in open desert west of Sidi Omar.

Graziani's instinct was to consolidate, but *Il Duce* grew frantic with impatience as the weeks went on. His African commander had to hit back hard and soon, he said. As the hapless 'Lucky' continued to hold back, Mussolini's anger only mounted: on 7 September, he told Graziani to attack or be dismissed.

OPERATION ANTICLIMAX

On 13 September, Italy's 10th Army spilled across the frontier from Libya into Egypt. Quickly, they advanced along the country's northern coast. The aim of *Operazione E*, as it was codenamed, was the seizure of the Suez Canal, a vital link between the Mediterranean and the Indian Ocean and, for Britain, a crucial connection with the wider Commonwealth.

For the sort of sustained attack needed to dislodge British forces from the Canal Zone, the Italians would need to be well supplied and equipped, and that meant the construction of a modern road. The late Italo Balbo's coast road – the *Litoranea Balbo* or *Via Balbia* – had

THE AIM OF *OPERAZIONE E* WAS THE SEIZURE OF THE SUEZ CANAL, A VITAL LINK BETWEEN THE MEDITERRANEAN AND THE INDIAN OCEAN.

Below: Italian troops in North Africa – like these anti-aircraft gunners – were experienced and well-trained. The problem throughout the campaign was keeping them supplied.

1962) as 'a tactician's paradise, a quartermaster's hell'. The only road here was the *Litoranea Balbo* along the coast, and this was quickly reduced to rubble in certain sections by weeks of fighting.

Off-road – that is, through practically the whole of Libya – although the vast expanses of empty sand that stretched away inland might appear inviting, they could be difficult to negotiate for untracked vehicles. Tanks fared better; as the thrilling newsreel footage from the conflict shows, this was in some ways the ideal arena for them.

SO FAR THE GREATEST INROADS THEY HAD MADE HAD BEEN ON THE ITALIAN – AND, TO A LESSER EXTENT, THE GERMAN – NAVAL CODES.

To a considerable extent, then, the Desert War, especially at this stage, was a war over control of the coast. Inland areas were only secondarily important. From the Allied point of view, the capture of Tobruk was doubly important: not only did they gain a port but the Italians were denied one.

After that, the Commonwealth troops pushed on in pursuit of what was now a headlong Italian retreat along the *Litoranea Balbo* towards the next big port, Benghazi. Its capture seemed to cement the Allied hold on Cyrenaica securely, while the Italian retreat along the coast road continued pell-mell. While the main body of Wavell's army pressed them in the rear, the 7th Armoured Division (later celebrated as the 'Desert Rats') was sent across country to cut off these fleeing forces. After the Battle of Beda Fomm (6–7 February), they were stopped and some 25,000 taken prisoner.

ULTRA-IRRELEVANT?

All this was happening without any particular reference to Bletchley Park. So far, the war was progressing quite well without ULTRA. Deciphered codes had given top leadership confidence in some situations and endorsed the odd decision already made. While not negligible, it was not essential. The secrecy with which this decrypted intelligence was necessarily surrounded only made things worse, as we've seen. When the information *was* good, it often seemed too important to be used. The rest of the time it came late, or with too little context to make sense.

It would have helped if the codebreakers had been able to triangulate their findings, comparing it with information gleaned from other sources. So far, though, the greatest inroads they had made had been on the Italian – and, to a lesser extent, the German – naval codes. The more sophisticated *Abwehr* (Germany Military Intelligence) code was proving more resistant.

There is a good reason, then, that ULTRA's first great triumph was to come at sea and involve the Italian fleet. As we return to the early months of 1941 and the run-up to Cape Matapan, we see this weak point in the Axis defences as an emerging theme. If ULTRA was to loom larger from now on in the overall narrative of the North Africa campaign, this owed to the importance of sea-borne supplies and logistical support in the Desert War.

Below: An Italian field-gun crew surveys the surrounding desert. The presence of so much empty space was at once an opportunity and a challenge.

An ULTRA intercept of 9 February 1941 suggested that German troops were being carried in numbers in that week's Naples–Tripoli convoys. This seemed so unlikely it was ignored. Again, it is clear that Bletchley Park faced a challenge not just in decrypting the coded communications it received but in its own communications with the leadership in London (and theirs with commanders in the field). Until they were all in the habit of taking ULTRA information seriously, it would not be able to prove its worth – but until it proved its worth, it wouldn't get their attention.

The new German arrivals heading southwards crossed at sea with British soldiers being shipped northwards to lend support in Greece. Their work in North Africa was just about done, it was

AN ENIGMA AND A HALF

THE ENIGMA MACHINE USED by the *Abwehr* (German military intelligence) was more sophisticated than those that Dilly Knox and his Bletchley Park codebreakers had cracked so far. Every Enigma machine had a 'reflector' – an electronically wired panel that turned back the electrical impulses sent it via the different contacts around the machine's revolving rotors. As the input text was encrypted by the sender, the reflector returned it in its scrambled form – or, of course, decrypted for the reader.

In most service machines this reflector was fixed, although a hand-crank in the commercial model allowed it to be moved each day to eliminate a layer of predictability. The *Abwehr* Enigma took this an important stage further: it was set up so that its wiring changed automatically in use, causing the rotors to go through

one or more 'turn-overs' in mid-encryption, introducing a new level of complexity to the code. An already mind-boggling problem was given a whole new dimension of difficulty: for Knox, this was a source of fascination. Spotting that certain recurrent patterns of relations between letters kept cropping up (he called them 'crabs'), he guessed that less often (and so more revealingly) half-crabs (or, as he named them, 'lobsters') might occur.

Setting his staff on a 'lobster hunt' in the messages they had, Knox was able to work back from their finds to deduce the number of rotor settings and the sorts of sequences they followed. By October 1941, they had come up with a convincing account of the workings of the *Abwehr* Enigma. Even then, it was not until 8 December that they deciphered their first message.

believed; they could be spared to help out in southeastern Europe and the Balkans.

ENTER ERWIN

The arrival in Tripoli of *Generalleutnant* Erwin Rommel (1891–1944) on 12 February was not seen as a special event. The new commander's name became known through intercepted messages, but the cult around the 'Desert Fox' had yet to arise. Rommel had distinguished himself, as far as his superiors were concerned, as a dashing tank commander in the Battle of France, but his reputation in the world outside the *Wehrmacht* was still to be made. In the days that followed, Rommel was attended by the reinforcing divisions that were destined to become known

Above: Not only did the rotors move in this *Abwehr* Enigma machine, but the reflector (right) went round in steps as well.

HOME-FROM-HOME FRONT

Woburn Abbey made a surprisingly uncomfortable billet for Bletchley staff.

BLETCHLEY PARK WAS ITSELF a house, of course, but that didn't mean anyone could live there. Every available room was quickly taken up as office space. The first few staff to arrive – the 'shooting party' – were quite easily accommodated in nearby inns and guesthouses. But as Bletchley Park expanded, housing became more problematic. Soon it was to be a running crisis.

It was exacerbated by the fact that the 'boffins' weren't to be Bletchley's only incomers: soon evacuees were being brought here from Blitz-hit parts of London. Before the war, the town's population had hovered somewhere just below the 7,000 mark; by the beginning of 1941, it was approaching 11,000.

Many workers were housed at Woburn Abbey, where they lived in considerable splendour but some discomfort: 'the food was awful ... bad eggs and fish with maggots in it', one woman recalled.

Maggots may be non-negotiable, but other factors were more relative: attitudes to catering at Bletchley and in its associated billets varied to some extent according to the individual's personal temperament and tastes and social background. Whilst some felt wretched, chewing away at bad or at best insipid food, others were excited to find normally rationed items readily available here – fresh salad, to give just one little example.

Others were billeted on local families – some willing, some reluctant, but just about all extremely curious about their work. For some, inevitably, there were culture-shocks: hopelessly learned, bookishly bashful young scholars forced to make small-talk with gruff railwaymen or farmworkers; delicately-nurtured young ladies rubbing shoulders with shopgirls and hairdressers. But then that could be educative all-round; in any case, it was the way it was for everyone in World War II.

as the *Afrika Korps*, and this drew the attention of the Allied leadership. Wavell would be seriously outnumbered now. That said, he had been seriously outnumbered before, and the forces that had outnumbered him were being registered as POWs at that very time. Like its commander's, the *Afrika Korps*' mystique was yet to be formed.

ULTRA was coming good around now; a great deal of information was becoming available on the movements of troops and equipment that would enable Operation *Sonnenblume* ('Sunflower') to proceed. The German plan was to fix the mess the Italians had made of Libya. Rommel and his men were, first, to reinforce those Italian troops remaining in the country's western half and protect Tripolitania and its capital. (Later, if it should become possible once further reinforcements had arrived, attempts might be made to claw back some of the lost territory.)

Below: Rommel, in iconic pose, standing in his staff car in the desert. But his North African foray was ultimately to end in failure.

Neither Wavell nor Churchill was unduly concerned at the new arrivals: Britain's strategic position in North Africa was much stronger than it had been, with the possession of key ports along the coast. Frankly, they were complacent. By Wavell's own admission: 'I had certainly not budgeted for Rommel after my experience of the Italians,' he confessed.

ULTRA ON-STREAM

The news from Bletchley Park was becoming harder to ignore; Wavell received the first of a growing stream of ULTRA information on 14 March. Five days later, the announcement

BLETCHLEY DOES ITS BIT

MEANWHILE, BACK IN BLETCHLEY, life was going on in that same strange wartime-British way, with a regime that combined the crashingly mundane with the heroic. Morale had to be kept up, of course; and so it was, the *North Bucks Times* for 14 January, 1941, revealing that – war or no war – 'The Parent's Association of the Bletchley Road Schools' had 'held a social evening in Bletchley Road school hall.' The giddy round went on: just four weeks later, the local paper led with the news that the Bletchley Road Schools' Parents' Association had 'held a social evening for the Spitfire Fund'.

And so it went on: if it wasn't diphtheria inoculations, it was a 'Ship Adoption' social (the school sponsored the freighter *SS Cheswell*, and duly received a visit from her captain). Or the appearance of local conjurer Bernard Brown, who delighted his audience by pulling 'a pile of carrots and a string of sausages' from the pocket of the local council chairman. He too appeared on the stage in the school hall. But the conflict was never far from people's thoughts: even crafts and hobbies were directed towards the War Effort, as Headmaster, Mr E. Cook, was to explain:

Due to the war, in addition to the usual activities, a knitting guild has been started with around 400 garments despatched to the Forces. Most of the wool came from voluntary subscriptions from children and staff and free wool would be issued once the school had proved its worth.

But then the war was never that far away, in fact: one of the highlights of the school year was the exhibition of a downed Me 109 in the school grounds, which raised the sum of £51, said the *North Bucks Times*. 'Souvenir hunters got away with small bits of fabric, but the vigilance of the Committee and helpers prevented further damage.'

that all air force leave in Africa had been cancelled made him sit up, while the day after that (20 March) he learned that a photo-reconnaissance sweep was being made over his front line.

A week before the Battle of Cape Matapan, Wavell was starting to sense the significance of this new intelligence source – though what it was telling him was unsettling. 'The situation on the Cyrenaica frontier,' he said in one dispatch, 'is causing me some anxiety, as growing enemy strength may indicate early forward movement. If our advanced troops are driven from present positions there is no good covering position south of Benghazi as country is dead level plain.'

Although Wavell continued to be cheered by the thought that logistical problems would limit the scope of any German fightback, he could see that his position now was not ideal.

If ULTRA was starting to prove its worth, however, it was revealing limitations too – specifically, the inability of *any* system to allow for the 'Rommel factor'. The general's orders were quite clear; correspondingly, so were the ULTRA transcripts. He was to

Above: Desert-dirtied German soldiers march in the direction of El Alamein – not to be the happiest of places for Rommel's troops.

Above: Panzer III tanks on the move in Tunisia. Though starved of supplies, they still held the Allied advance for several months.

remain in a defensive posture for the time being, at very least until the arrival of the 15th Panzer Division, which wasn't scheduled to happen for a few months. Wavell, his superiors said, could be sure that nothing of importance would happen before 1 May.

On 24 March, however, Rommel's tanks beat the British at El Agheila, on the Gulf of Sidra; a week later they were advancing on Benghazi. It was the Allies who were caught napping now: on 4 April, Benghazi had fallen to the Axis; by 10 April, Tobruk was under siege. Rommel was leading an onward thrust towards the Egyptian border – a bold stroke, and one he would subsequently think better of. It rattled Wavell and his forces, though, especially when four days later Rommel reached the border town of Sallum and occupied the strategic Halfaya Pass.

TOBRUK UNTAKEN
Rommel's regrets over having left business unfinished at Tobruk were well founded. As we've seen, access to seaborne supplies was crucial to the conduct of the Desert War, and

impetuosity really cost him now; his eastward advance lost its impetus as the difficulty in securing rations, parts and munitions began to bite. Keeping it was to be costly for the Allies, in lives, ships and resources; a succession of attempts to relieve the siege were frustrated through the months that followed. But the price paid by the Germans was to be much higher, so many hundreds of miles from Tripoli and wholly reliant on the tenuous supply route through a beleaguered Benghazi.

Thanks to ULTRA, moreover, this difficulty was known to Allied chiefs, who had been able to read a report sent back to Berlin by General Friedrich Paulus (1890–1957). A couple of years later, his surrender at Stalingrad was to enrage the *Führer*; his news now wasn't much more encouraging. Rommel's position, he said, was weak and he was critically short of fuel and ammunition. Hitler's reaction is not reported, but Churchill was delighted.

Below: German transport stands outside the port city of Tobruk. Fought over as a strategic port for a conflict which hinged on logistics, Tobruk was to take a real hammering in the war.

FROM BREVITY TO BATTLEAXE

There is the sense of a pendulum swing in the way we see ULTRA intelligence being handled at this time. Just a few months before, it had been ignored. By March, however, its suggestion that Rommel would be staying put was being taken as holy writ – and now Paulus' report was prompting Churchill to overplay his hand.

He wasn't going to bear the blame, though. Now it was Wavell's turn to feel the kind of pressure Graziani had before him to mount an offensive he wasn't really ready for. Operation Brevity began on 15 May. It was aptly named, being over in just over 24 hours, by which time Brigadier-General William Gott (1897–1942) had succeeded in one of his objectives – securing the Halfaya Pass – but failed in the other, taking back Fort Capuzzo. Within a fortnight, in any case, the Germans had reoccupied the pass and dug in with 88mm (3.46in) anti-aircraft guns: British airmen were to call it 'Hellfire Pass' from this time on.

A second, larger-scale, offensive, Operation Battleaxe (15–17 June), ended in a bad defeat for Wavell. The British lost almost a thousand men and nearly a hundred tanks. Wavell lost his job – a little unfairly; his replacement General Claude Auchinleck (1884–1981) was no more eager than his predecessor had been to press his perceived (by Churchill) advantage and attack.

RUSSIAN RELIEF

Auchinleck was to find himself fortunate in the timing of his arrival. By 22 June, Operation Barbarossa was under way in Eastern Europe. Hitler's invasion of the Soviet Union

Below: Field Marshal Archibald Wavell (left) talks tactics with General Claude Auchinleck – who was so soon to replace him in command.

OPERATION FLIPPER

15 NOVEMBER 1941 WAS Rommel's fiftieth birthday and British commandos had a brutal surprise in store. Plans were drawn up for a night raid on his Libyan headquarters at Beda Littoria. There, it was assumed, the already talismanic general might be assassinated, while nearby wireless and communications installations could also be destroyed.

In fact, the thinking behind the attack seems to have been less about spoiling the festive fun than on helping Operation Crusader off to the best possible start. Just as well, given that ULTRA intelligence had already tracked the general's plans to be away from 1 November for a few weeks' R&R with his wife Lucie in Rome.

Flipper flopped. Most of the attackers were quickly captured; a couple were killed and only three escaped. In any case, it subsequently emerged, Rommel hadn't used Beda Littoria as his base for some time. Later, the question was asked whether the raiders had been hung out to dry to protect ULTRA's secrecy. This was by no means impossible.

meant a large-scale redistribution of resources for the German military machine, and a major shift of focus for the *Luftwaffe*. This evened things out on the battlefield a little, and made life easier for the British when it came to attacking Rommel's supply convoys, whether from the sea or the air.

That October, a special convoy-hunting fleet, 'Force K', was set up in Malta. Blenheim bombers gave it air support. ULTRA intelligence allowed its attacks to be carefully targeted. In what was becoming a tried-and-tested tactic (see Chapter 3), a 'chance sighting' by a spy-plane over the sea off the coast of Calabria on 8 October allowed the origins of information on the course of the 'Duisburg Convoy' to be concealed. So-called for its largest ship, the *Duisburg*, this group was carrying vital supplies for the *Afrika Korps* and their Italian allies. Seven merchant ships were sunk, along with an Italian destroyer, the *Fulmine*, with no British losses.

As the weeks went by, the British were able to build their strength, while Rommel's was to remain constant at very best.

By November, he had 414 tanks, 320 aircraft and nine divisions (only three of them German). Four of his divisions were tied down at Tobruk. The British by now had some 700 tanks, a thousand planes and eight divisions.

AN INCONCLUSIVE CRUSADE

The next attempt to lift the Siege of Tobruk would fare no better than its predecessors. Operation Crusader began on 18 November. Led by Lieutenant General Alan Cunningham (1887–1983), Britain's Eighth Army advanced on the Halfaya Pass; meanwhile, the Thirtieth and Thirteenth Army Corps swept south and west to come at Tobruk from the other side. They got as far as Sidi Rezegh, 32km (20 miles) southeast of the besieged seaport before Rommel attacked them in the rear with a couple of panzer divisions. The move was designed to take some of the pressure off his forces in the Halfaya Pass and to separate the Eighth Army from its support.

The result was inconclusive – so a great deal better for Rommel than for the British commanders. He'd certainly drawn the sting out of their attack. Cunningham faced a near-mutiny from his officers when he called for the operation – now badly compromised – to be cancelled. Auchinleck agreed and a few days later sacked him for his caution. As accurate as Cunningham's assessment might have been, his superior's strategy was to be vindicated when, on 29 November, the British broke through to Tobruk.

As victories go, this was a ragged one, but Auchinleck was understandably glad to take a win. Historians have for the most part seen Crusader's aftermath as a missed opportunity. Rommel's strength might have been completely crushed, it is argued. In the event, the weeks that followed saw him put on a tactical masterclass – albeit one aimed primarily at damage limitation and survival.

ROMMEL ON THE ROPES

In November (thanks in considerable part to ULTRA information on Axis convoy movements), less than a quarter of the supplies

Opposite: British anti-aircraft guns fend off German attackers at Tobruk, which withstood a 241-day siege from Rommel's forces in 1941.

'ACTION THIS DAY'

THE CHALLENGE FACING BLETCHLEY PARK at first had been to find some way of cracking the Enigma codes. To a great degree that challenge had been met. More problematic was the struggle of a small staff to cope with the volume of encrypted intelligence they were being asked to handle. By the autumn of 1941, with Dilly's unlocking of the *Abwehr* code, the stream of communications looked like becoming a vast tide.

Its character as a close little community of minds may have stood Bletchley Park in good stead to begin with. Now, though, it threatened to nullify its work. If the codebreakers couldn't get through sufficient messages at sufficient speed, they would be left hopelessly in arrears as events unfolded. Hence the decision of a leading group – including Gordon Welchman, Hugh Alexander, Stuart Milner-Barry and Alan Turing – to write their own top-secret but urgent letter to Churchill. The prime minister had visited Bletchley Park a few

weeks previously and showered praise on its work.

'We think, however,' the signatories of this letter now warned him, 'that you ought to know that this work is being held up, and in some cases is not being done and principally because we cannot get sufficient staff to deal with it. Our reason for writing to you direct is that we have done everything that we possibly can through the normal channels, and that we despair of any early improvement without your intervention.'

That intervention would not be slow in coming. Churchill reportedly immediately wrote the order 'Action this Day':

Make sure they have all they want on extreme priority and report to me that this has been done.

Soon the staff at Bletchley Park had been supplemented by a veritable fleet of Wrens (Women's Royal Navy Service) and the bombes were working away, cracking code on an industrial scale.

shipped out from Italy had made it to North Africa. The *Afrika Korps* was running on empty, it appeared.

However, it wasn't over yet. The Germans still controlled a vast area of territory in western Libya and Rommel was securely established in Tripoli. But supplies were still a problem. The port of Tripoli could handle only five big cargo ships – some 44,000 tons of freight – a month under optimum conditions. And these weren't optimum conditions, by any means.

FRUSTRATION

By May 1942, Rommel felt ready to strike again. Defeating the Eighth Army at the Battle of Gazala (26–27 May), he went on to retake Tobruk. The *Abwehr* code had by now been broken, and ULTRA intelligence flowed much more plentifully; even so, the information it provided was often exasperatingly partial. This was the case with the latest attack: that an attack was imminent had been obvious; where it would be and how conducted had been less clear.

The problems in managing the information went on as well, and not just the old dilemma of which bits to use and which deliberately to pass over for the sake of maintaining secrecy. Having so much secret information circulating, with so few people cleared to handle it, had created logjams that were causing new delays. And those with sufficient security clearance were – almost by definition – remote from the places in which

Below: WRENS were to become a mainstay of working life at Bletchley Park. Over 2,500 would be working there by the end of the war.

Above: British
artillerymen keep up a
steady bombardment at
El Alamein. The fighting
here would mark a turning
point in the Desert War.

events were actually unfolding, with no comprehension of the
specific conditions there.

It seemed like two steps forward, one step back; each
improvement in the system brought new problems. Overall,
though, things were heading in the right direction. The results
were starting to be registered on the battlefield as well, although
Rommel remained a formidable threat. Indeed, by the end of
June 1942 he had pushed the British back across the border into
Egypt. He showed every inclination to go further, on to Suez, but
a determined stand by the Eighth Army finally held his advance
at the First Battle of El Alamein (1–27 July).

A few months later (23 October–11 November), El Alamein
was to be the scene of a second battle, widely seen as the turning
point in the Desert War. The new commander of the Eighth
Army, General Bernard Law Montgomery (1887–1976), was
well armed with information on the numbers and disposition of
the Axis forces. Although the victory was Monty's and his men's,
there is no doubt that ULTRA helped.

CARRYING A TORCH

By now, the ULTRA system seemed to be running smoothly: for the first time, the codebreakers could feel they were on top of things, the information that they harnessed quickly and efficiently distributed. When plans began to be put in place for Operation Torch, the joint British–US invasion of North Africa through Morocco, Algeria and Tunisia – so well to the west of Libya – ULTRA intelligence was able to play a vital part. Its first task was to provide reassurance that the Germans hadn't discovered the plan. Consistently, the message came through that they had not. Decrypted transcripts from Franco's Spain meanwhile made clear that, unenthusiastic as the Generalissimo might be about Allied forces tramping through 'his' colony of Morocco, he wouldn't see it as something to sacrifice his neutral status over.

The co-operation of Vichy France had also to be secured – or at least that of tractable representatives in Algeria. This would need the most careful handling; some officials seemed likely to be more amenable (or, as Pétain and Hitler might have put it – 'disloyal') than others. Either way it was risky: again, careful monitoring from Bletchley offered reassurance that none of the contacts Allied agents had made had reported their approaches home.

So, on 8–19 November, three separate task forces

Below: The Second Battle of El Alamein (23 October–11 November 1942). Montgomery's main attack, to the north, was accompanied by secondary thrusts further south.

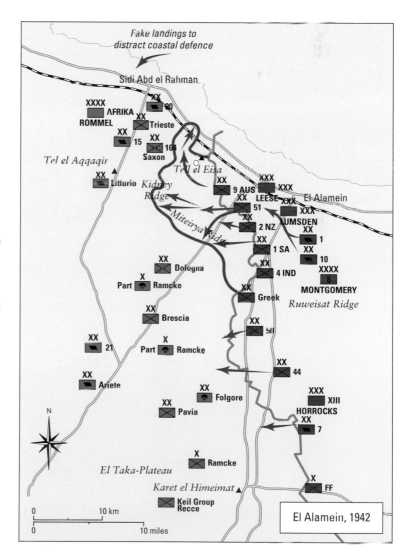

El Alamein, 1942

COLOMBO COMES THROUGH

It had for some time made sense for GC&CS to have its outstations in the wider world. The FECB (Far East Combined Bureau) had long been established in Hong Kong. Since the Japanese invasion of China, though, it had been a bit more nomadic. By the beginning of 1942 it was in Colombo, Ceylon (now Sri Lanka).

It was very quickly to prove its worth. On 28 March 1942, Japanese signals were intercepted that suggested an imminent attack on the island. A fast carrier task force – six aircraft carriers strong, with other vessels in attendance – was on its way under the command of Admiral Chūchi Nagumo (1887–1944). The Japanese appeared to be intending a sort of 'Second Pearl Harbor' surprise on what was then an important centre for British military and merchant shipping in the Indian Ocean.

A little recklessly, given his orders at all costs to keep his fleet 'in being', Admiral Sir James Somerville (1882–1949) set out with a naval flotilla from Addu Atoll, the secret base of Britain's Eastern Fleet in the Maldives. His intention was to cut off the attack, but ultimately he cruised around for several days without finding any Japanese ships and, assuming that the FECB's codebreakers had got things wrong, he returned to Addu.

However, on 4 April the Japanese task force was sighted from the air. Somerville set off again with 48 ships – but by now he was too late to be of any help. Fortunately, however, Admiral Geoffrey Layton (1884–1964), in command in Colombo, had the presence of mind to order the evacuation and dispersal of all the shipping that was crowded into Colombo harbour.

The Japanese fleet, including the aircraft carriers *Zuikaku* and *Akagi*, in the Indian Ocean, March 1942.

landed, from ships and from the air by parachute: one in the
west, in Morocco, at Fedala (Casablanca), and at Safi and Port
Lyautey to the south and north. The second, centre, task force
landed near Oran, in Algeria; the third not far from the country's
capital, Algiers. General Dwight D. Eisenhower (1890–1969) was
in overall command of what might be seen as an early rehearsal
for D-Day (6 June 1944): certainly, he was to learn from some of
the mistakes made here.

Above: Fresh American
troops come ashore on
the coast of North Africa
in one of the three main
landings that launched
Operation Torch.

ULTRA UNSTUCK?

Is it fair to blame ULTRA for the sense of invulnerability it may
sometimes have seemed to confer? The landing at Fedala met
much tougher resistance from French troops based there than
had been expected. The one at Oran, though largely unopposed,
nearly did for itself thanks to planning oversights – the water was
much shallower than expected, farther out from shore. Again,
we get the sense that military planners were struggling to find a
satisfactory middle ground between disregarding ULTRA and
seeing it as a solution to all problems.

Then, too, there were the sorts of problems that arise
whenever complex plans with shifting variables are made.

The most accurate data becomes 'wrong' immediately the context changes. ULTRA information that suggested that, in the event of the early October invasion originally envisaged for Operation Torch, Hitler would either write off North Africa completely or rush in token reinforcements became moot once the decision was made to put it back by some six weeks. Indeed, ULTRA intelligence had specifically stated that, in the event of a November 'Torch', the Germans – freed from the fear of an

OPERATION SATIN

SOME OF THE STRENGTHS – and limitations – of ULTRA intelligence in application are evident in the planning of the abandoned Operation Satin (January 1943).

Chafing impatiently in Tunis and eager for action, Eisenhower came up with a plan to chase Rommel down in southern Tunisia, where, loosely cornered by Britain's Eighth Army, he'd decided to lie low through the rainy winter months. It was drier, more fit for fighting, in the uplands there. Although he recognized that a direct attack on Rommel was not realistic, Eisenhower hoped an American force might turn up the pressure by attacking important points on the German supply line. He wanted his 1st Armored Division to sweep eastward across the centre of the country from Gafsa towards the Mediterranean, to the ports of Sfax and Gabès or the vital airfield of Kairouan, further inland.

But how was Eisenhower's attack itself to be supplied? To ensure the necessary speed, the 1st Armored would have to travel light. Should all go well, this would

hardly matter: there would be supplies to spare in the bases they were about to take. But there was no significant margin for error: ULTRA intelligence was vital in

A German Panzer III grinds its way across a bridge in a Tunisian town.

Allied assault across the English Channel in the winter months – would feel able to offer more significant resistance.

So it proved, ULTRA again coming through with dispiriting accuracy in its reports on Germany's impressive mobilization to prevent an Allied advance through Tunisia. In the event, Eisenhower called a halt to Torch in Tunis, kept there by the winter rains and a more menacing than expected Axis presence to the east.

allowing the necessary decisions to be made.

First, the green light: for the moment, it seemed, Rommel was reasonably firmly pinned down by Montgomery's force. The Americans would only have to contend with the 5th Panzer Army, led by Hans-Jürgen von Arnim (1889–1962). They, too, were relatively recent arrivals in North Africa. ULTRA intercepts assessed Von Arnim's army's strength at some 75,000 men. It didn't give a figure for the amount of armour, but a bit of creativity with the decrypted unloading records for the ports of Tunis and Bizerte allowed Bletchley Park to come up with a figure of 200 tanks – just half a dozen out, a later decrypt would reveal.

Next, however, came the bad news: subsequent ULTRA decrypts indicated that – Montgomery or no Montgomery – Rommel planned to send his 21st Panzers towards Sfax. By 15 January, further decrypts confirmed that these men and tanks were on the move. Eisenhower didn't

General von Arnim meets his men. Axis forces in Tunisia weren't as war-weary as Eisenhower had hoped.

fancy the chances of his freshly landed troops against these seasoned veterans. Operation Satin was discreetly shelved.

If this episode once again underscores the value of ULTRA intelligence, it underlines its limitations too. Certain things simply won't come up in message transcripts. On paper, 5th and 21st Panzer were broadly similar in strength; in practice, Eisenhower realized that wasn't so.

Above: American troops trudge down a dusty road in the Kasserine Pass, the scene of an inglorious defeat for the Allied army.

At least, however, the operation had increased the difficulties facing an already hard-pressed Rommel. At sea, the stranglehold on his supplies was tightening. Again, ULTRA-originated information was assisting the Royal Navy and RAF. Just about enough was getting through to maintain the Panzer army through September and October, it appears. In December, though, less than 13,000 tons left Italy, and less than half of this got through. As of 14 December, the *Afrika Korps* had only enough fuel to take it 50km (30 miles) in all. Rommel's army was there for the taking.

KASSERINE CARVE-UP

ULTRA was to be in the dock again after (on 17–19 February) an Anglo-American army was badly beaten defending western Tunisia's Kasserine Pass. The Operation Torch troops involved on the Allied side were recent arrivals in North Africa, and ill-equipped to face the hardened veterans on the German side.

Criticism was also made of the unimaginative leadership of Lloyd Fredendall (1883–1963) and Kenneth Anderson (1891–1959), who were slow to react to a well-nigh overwhelming attack by Von Arnim's forces. There's no doubt, though, that they'd all been let down by their intelligence. Although clear on the fact that a German attack in strength was imminent, Bletchley Park had suggested that it would come further to the north through the Pichon-Fondouk Pass.

This might not have mattered so much if more trouble had been taken to cross-check ULTRA intelligence with that from other sources – especially from observation on the ground. Again, the temptation at the top was to see this decrypted material as trumping what was happening in the field. As Brigadier General Staff for Intelligence Sir Kenneth Strong (1900–82) acknowledged:

Accurate reports of the strength and direction of the impending attack had been sent from the front but it appears that they had been discounted both at First Army Headquarters and Allied Force Headquarters, as being an exaggeration on the part of green and untried troops.

ULTRA to some extent redeemed itself in the aftermath of Kasserine. The German commanders lost time disputing where their next attack should be. The flurry of encrypted dispatches this meant was meat and drink to the codebreakers – and the days of grace allowed the Allies to bring in reinforcements on the ground. Assisted by new intelligence, they were able to go on the offensive and snatch a significant victory from what had been a disastrous rout.

'ALL THE DIFFERENCE'
'A few hours might make all the difference,' the decrypt of 28 November 1943 said. The 15th and 21st Panzer Divisions were both in desperate straits, out of

Below: 'Monty' (right) with General Harold Alexander: the Tunisian campaign was to be testing for commanders on both sides.

made something of a habit of it. A few months before, at Mareth, on 20 March, he'd chosen to attack the Mareth Line, north of Medenine, in a direct frontal attack. Not only had ULTRA intelligence made clear that this defensive fortification was formidably defended, but ground reconnaissance had shown it could be easily outflanked. Monty's wilfulness seems to have stemmed from his assumption that a predominantly Italian defensive force would quickly buckle and break. In the event, his initial assault was thrown back ignominiously and, although he did secure his victory in the end, it was much more hard-won than it need have been.

Below: In the end, ironically, the 'Desert War' was to be won and lost at sea: here anti-aircraft gunners protect an Allied convoy.

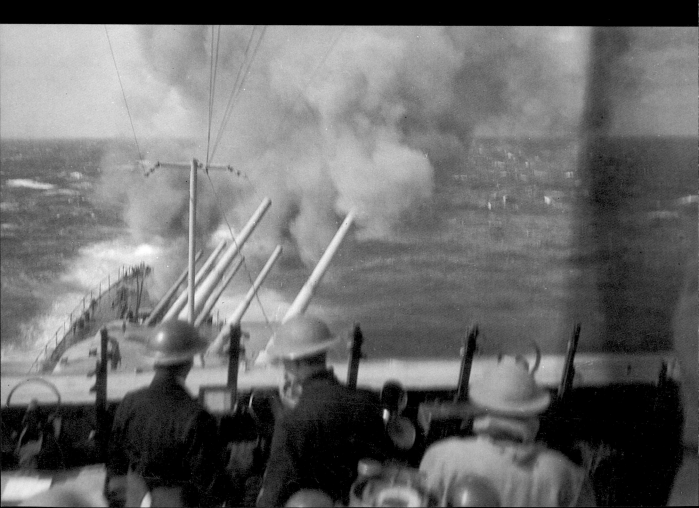

A TRIUMPH OF ATTRITION

A few more months, though, and it would all be over. Rommel's attack on the Eighth Army at Medenine (6 March) had been unavailing; from that time on, he was fighting an increasingly impossible rearguard action. A few days later, he was recalled to Europe, his role in North Africa over. General von Arnim was left to struggle on.

Ultimately, as the unfortunate 'Lucky' Graziani had realized, the Desert War was all about supplies. Rommel's dash and daring had certainly added a splash of colour and romance; over the months and weeks, though, even he had been worn down.

The Allied triumph was ultimately to be a victory for prosaic practicality over military flair. Maybe the moral of this story is that a backroom operation like Bletchley Park fares better when it contributes further behind the scenes. Although ULTRA intelligence had made its contribution on the battlefield, it had brought with it risks as well as advantages, introduced new possibilities of human error and raised needless anxieties or unwarranted confidence.

THE BEST INTELLIGENCE IS USELESS IF IT IS IGNORED. MONTGOMERY MADE SOMETHING OF A HABIT OF IT.

All this time, however, in allowing Allied naval and air forces to chip away at the Axis supply lines across the Mediterranean, it had slowly but surely been making victory inevitable. Thanks to Bletchley's codebreakers, the dates and dispositions of all the Axis convoys went straight to London. A coordinated attempt by Allied air forces to cut air supplies from Italian North Africa was orchestrated under Operation Flax (5–27 April), in which more than 400 Axis aircraft were shot down.

Meanwhile, the Royal Navy continued to pound the Mediterranean convoys on the water. Twenty-nine ships were sunk in April 1943 alone. That same month, of 34,000 tons of supplies embarked in Italy, only 18,000 made it to North Africa. By the beginning of May, the average figure for the amount of freight unloaded at Tunisia's various ports each day had dropped from 1300 to 700 tons. An intercepted message of 10 April complained that, rather than the 400 tons of fuel a day they

Above: In hindsight, *The Man Who Never Was* (1956) offered a prophetic glimpse of a new world of virtual realities, first brought into being at Bletchley Park.

needed, German forces were getting only 271 on average. They were, Von Arnim warned, facing 'complete supply breakdown'. The Axis campaign in Africa ended, not with a bang – nor even a whimper – but with the rasp and splutter of countless engines out of fuel.

INVASION OF SICILY

Sicily was to be the Allies' stepping stone to Italy and an attack on the soil of one of the Axis homelands. Bletchley Park was to play a vital role here as well. Always an 'unsung hero', it made its contribution with the most mundane intelligence – the distribution of German and Italian aircraft in southern Italy, for example; and bottlenecks in fuel supplies. Armed with information on these things, however, Allied commanders were able to make their plans in the knowledge that they were giving their troops the best possible chance of a successful landing.

Then, of course, to top things off, it was an ULTRA interception that confirmed the success of 'Operation Mincemeat' – better known, of course, as the story of 'The Man who Never Was'. The body of a homeless drifter found dead in a London warehouse was kitted out with his own new identity as Captain William Martin of the Royal Marines and authenticating papers, along with a convincing set of personal possessions. His body was left drifting with a briefcase full of documents designed to persuade the Germans and Italians that the plan was for a full-scale invasion of Europe from the southeast, from Sardinia and Greece, and that any manoeuvrings around Sicily were to be no more than a clever feint.

As cunning as it might have been, the Allies would have no real way of knowing that the Germans had taken the bait till Bletchley Park read as much in a decrypted message of 14 May 1943. Operation Husky went ahead – largely unhindered – on 9 July.

DENIABLE DESTRUCTION

THE NAVAL WAR IN the Mediterranean at this stage may have had something of the feel of an Allied shooting spree, but the need for care and discretion remained as great as ever. The trick with the Sunderland flying-boat which had worked so well in the lead-up to Cape Matapan now had to be replicated over and over across many thousands of square miles.

And it wasn't just the enemy that the ULTRA secret had to be protected from: even senior Allied personnel were not to know. The result was that, once again, their commanders had to 'play God', sending submariners and airmen here and there, so they could 'chance' upon their targets. As

Bletchley Park veteran, Sir F.H. ('Harry') Hinsley (1918–98) was later to explain:

Every one of those ships before it was sunk had to be sighted by a British aeroplane or submarine which had been put in a position where it would sight it without it knowing it had been placed in that position, and had made a sighting signal which the Germans and the Italians had intercepted. That was the standard procedure. As a consequence the Germans and the Italians assumed that we had 400 submarines whereas we had 25. And they assumed that we had a huge reconnaissance force on Malta, whereas we had, at one point, only three aeroplanes!

4

ATLANTIC WAR

A hidden menace, and more unsettling for that, the U-boats struck real fear into the Allied Command. It took a counter-weapon every bit as secretive to redress the military balance in the Atlantic.

I T IS NO TROPICAL lagoon: at latitude 58° North that would be too much to ask; the northernmost tip of the British mainland lies some 26km (16 miles) to the south. The gentlest breeze that ruffles these open waters can be unsettlingly chilly even at the height of summer; in winter, the cold can seem to cut to the bone. Seeing the oil tankers lined up here, though, you still get the sense of Scapa Flow as something of a sanctuary. It is unusual to see so vast and yet so sequestered a stretch of sea. Scapa Flow covers some 324 square kilometres (125 square miles).

Scapa Flow was the perfect anchorage, which is why Britain's Grand Fleet had its headquarters here during World War I. For centuries, the centre of activity for the Royal Navy had been Portsmouth, beside the Solent narrows on the south coast. With the Crimean War, and the rise of Imperial Russia, the geopolitical focus had shifted to the north. By the early years of the twentieth century, with German rearmament progressing rapidly and

Opposite: War between submarines and surface vessels was all cruel cat-and-mouse. Here a British ship drops depth charges in the North Atlantic.

war apparently inevitable, Scapa Flow took on this much more important role.

'INCREDIBLE...'

The 'Phony War' abruptly became real for this corner of Scotland just six weeks in, on 14 October 1939. In the early hours of the night of a high spring tide, with *Kapitanleutnant* Günther Prien (1908–41) at the wheel, on only his second patrol as commander, *U-47* stole through Kirk Sound into Scapa Flow. He sank HMS *Royal Oak* with a torpedo. Some 1400 men were on board when the battleship was hit, of whom 833 were lost; 120 of those were under the age of eighteen when their ship went down in 33m (108ft) of water.

This was a coup for commander and crew – still more, it seemed, for the Nazi news media, which reacted as though the war had now been won. Britain's much-vaunted naval power had been shown up as an apparent pretence; the nation of Drake

Below: A gunner's-eye-view of HMS *Hood*, at anchor in Orkney's Scapa Flow, sheltered from the worst of the weather on all sides.

and Nelson mocked and bullied. And just where, a few decades previously, the High Seas Fleet had gone to the bottom along with Germany's fortunes. If part of the purpose of the war, from the Nazis' point of view, was to restore the nation's dignity after the humiliations of 1918 and its aftermath, there could be no more fitting scene than Scapa Flow.

On *U-47*'s return to port, Prien was decorated by the *Führer* personally and lionized in newspapers and newsreels, which held him up as exemplifying all the warlike German virtues. Prien's incursion into Scapa Flow *had* undoubtedly been daring. Neutral observers could not help but be impressed. CBS's William L. Shirer (1904–93), sympathetic as he was to the British cause, struck an almost boyishly enthusiastic tone in his report: 'The place where the German U-boat sank the British battleship *Royal Oak* was none other than the middle of Scapa Flow, Britain's greatest naval base! It sounds incredible...'

Above: Fresh from its Scapa Flow success, *U-47* and its crew accept a well-earned salute from the battleship the *Scharnhorst*.

B-DIENST VS BAMS

WE SHOULD NOT ASSUME that the monitoring of signals traffic was one-sided. Bletchley Park's German counterpart, B-Dienst (the *Beobachtungsdienst* or 'observation service'), employed around a thousand codebreakers throughout the war. Pre-eminent among them was the inspirational Wilhelm Tranow. In keeping with his shadowy role, there are enormous gaps in this genius's known biography – including the years in which he was born and died. Trained as an engineer, he had served as a radio technician in World War I; it was then that he'd found his flair for breaking codes.

Much of Tranow's most important work was done on British signals. More than 800 B-Dienst staff were assigned to these. Under Tranow's leadership, they had real successes in deciphering the Royal Navy's various codes as the war went on: during the Norwegian Campaign, for instance, they are thought to have decrypted anything up to 50 per cent of British messages received.

By March 1940, B-Dienst were almost completely on top of the more straightforward BAMS (the British and Allied Merchant Ships' code), and German commanders were fully briefed on the comings and goings of the merchant shipping by which Britain hoped to keep itself supplied. As the year went on, they managed to penetrate more of the Royal Navy's codes. By the end of 1943, however, new British ciphers were brought in that they couldn't crack. The tide seemed to be turning, in cryptography as in the war.

BAD NEWS

The attack on Scapa Flow would sound less incredible a few years later after the Japanese Navy Air Service had attacked the US base at Pearl Harbor, Hawaii. For the moment, though, it seemed difficult to believe. Even allowing for the shortcomings in security that *U-47* had thrown into such high relief, it was a shock. So soon after the start of the war; so violent a blow at the heart of Britain's defences: it was news the nation didn't need to hear.

It was the kind of news the country would have to get used to, though. Three months later, just a few miles away, 189 men went down with the E-class destroyer HMS *Exmouth*, torpedoed while escorting a cargo ship some miles off Wick. This was another coup, given the size and significance of this British warship.

But such high-profile prizes weren't the whole U-boat story. By the time the *Exmouth* went down, well over a hundred British ships had been lost to U-boats. Overwhelmingly, these were merchant vessels. Cumulatively, though, these losses made a major dent in the British war effort. It wasn't just the sunken ships but the vital supplies that went down with them, and the way national morale went down in its turn. Altogether, the U-boat attacks were turning the screws on a people already starting to feel under siege.

Things got worse as 1940 went on: first, because early troubles with torpedo aiming and detonation mechanisms were resolved; second because, by the summer, the Germans were comfortably ensconced at France. Already a Baltic and a North Sea power, Germany now had immediate access to the Atlantic. Within weeks, heavily fortified U-boat pens were under construction at Brest and Saint-Nazaire. From there, submarines

Below: Coverage of the *Exmouth*'s sinking says a great deal for official openness – but it didn't do much for morale at a tricky time.

went out to ravage British merchant vessels in the Western Approaches and beyond; soon they threatened to establish a stranglehold. From August onwards, British ships were being sunk at a rate of around 40 every month. By October, the figure had risen to over 60. By the end of that month, it was becoming clear that the Battle of Britain had been won. But was the country to be starved into submission instead, by this blockade?

UNDERWATER, UNDERHAND

One of the less obvious impacts of World War II was the social mobility it engendered. We saw this with the stream of provincial scholarship boys arriving as recruits at Bletchley Park, and in the new importance attributed to what would once have seemed

Below: Germany's U-boats were just about invulnerable in port, safe and snug in specially-constructed reinforced concrete pens.

Above: Admiral Dönitz (centre) was destined to go right to the top in the Nazi state – albeit only in the days of its defeat.

inglorious 'back-room' work. These things were also happening in Germany to some extent. Hitler himself came from a humble background, and although he's hardly to be seen as the man who put the merit into meritocracy, he did help shift some long-established snobberies.

Karl Dönitz (1891–1980), despite his Nazi loyalties, makes a more convincing example. He was brought up outside Berlin, an engineer's son. Enlisting in the Navy in World War I, he ended up commanding a U-boat at a time when this wasn't considered the thing for an officer of the old school. By its nature, the submarine lurked and hid and took unfair advantage, creeping up to ambush the enemy. So invaluable had it proven in World War I, however, that the most conservative reluctantly had to acknowledge the U-boat's role.

Placed in charge of the U-boat fleet in 1939, Dönitz did not just shrug off the sneers; he embraced them and even doubled down. Rather than being used to engage enemy warships, he insisted, they should be deployed against merchant shipping as a matter of strategy. These were the softest of targets, and this was the least glorious way of waging war. This would barely even qualify as fighting as far as the harrumphing elders of the *Kriegsmarine* were concerned.

As Dönitz had promised, though, the strategy of interrupting supplies played havoc with the Allies' ability to fight, and came excruciatingly close to winning Germany the war. So delighted was the *Führer* with his U-boat commander that he ultimately made Dönitz his designated successor. So it was that, for a few weeks after Hitler's suicide at the end of April 1945, Admiral Dönitz served as President of Germany and Supreme Commander of Armed Forces.

ONCE A TARGET HAD BEEN SIGHTED, HALF-HOURLY UPDATES WERE NEEDED TO MARSHAL THE GATHERING U-BOATS.

'HAPPY TIME'

For U-boat commanders and their crews, this period of picking off Allied shipping with virtual impunity came to be known as the 'Happy Time'. Admiral Karl Dönitz commanded the U-boat fleet; it was his idea, in the latter part of 1940, to form them into what he called 'wolf packs'. The idea was that they would keep in close contact both with one another and with their base (and hence, ultimately, with him) so that their attacks might be more closely coordinated.

Tactics both for cruising and for final attack changed as well. Until now, the U-boats had roamed singly, searching for a target, submerging on the sight of an Allied vessel so as to be able to 'stalk' it, then coming up again once within range to begin firing. Now, when he saw a potential target, a skipper was supposed to notify his fellow submariners – and Dönitz, back at his base at Kernével Harbour, near Lorient, southeast of Brest. Only when the other pack members were in the best possible positions and Admiral Dönitz had ordered the attack was he permitted to fire his first torpedo. What had been a haphazard every-skipper-for-himself approach was now a highly sophisticated operation, and devastatingly effective. Dönitz's reforms transformed the U-boat from a nuisance to a serious scourge; perhaps even a war-winning weapon for the Germans.

A price had to be paid for the smooth running of this system: communication. The amount of signals traffic went up and up. Previously, the U-boat skipper had been expected to dispatch no more than a daily location report; now he was supposed to check in with his superiors much more often. Once a target had been sighted and other pack members alerted, half-hourly updates were needed so that the gathering U-boats could be sufficiently closely marshalled. Even as it optimized the wolf pack's attacking approach, the resulting flurry of signals created a vulnerability to interception, Dönitz realized. At least it would have done, were it not for the Enigma and its codes.

As of summer 1940, that confidence was justified. Despite significant progress at Bletchley Park against the Germans' Army

Below: Otto Kretschmer (1912–98), seen on the right here on the lookout for another kill, was among the most successful U-boat commanders.

STEALTH STRATEGY

Submarine warfare was inherently modern: even so, by now it had a history. The Confederacy's *H.L. Hunley* had sunk the Union sloop *Housatonic* in the American Civil War (1864). Its German history was particularly rich: though they'd dived only for short stints for concealment and had to surface before they attacked, an early wave of U-boats had proven a potent weapon in World War I. It remained the case well into World War II that the U-boat submerged only to stalk its target or when pursued during the daytime: given sonar, it could hide more easily on the surface after dark. While the widespread use of the snorkel from about 1943 allowed it to remain underwater longer, this was primarily as a defensive strategy, to avoid detection.

and Air Force Codes, the Naval Code ('Dolphin') was proving resistant, even with Alan Turing on the case with his brilliant colleague Peter Twinn (1916–2004) working day in, day out with the assistance of one of the first.

Previous breakthroughs had been made with the assistance of windfall finds like those on the trawlers *Polares* and *Krebs*. Something of the sort would be needed now; Operation Ruthless was intended to force the issue.

THE 'BATTLE' BEGINS

Time was not on Bletchley's side: as summer gave way to autumn, the U-boats continued to tighten the screw on Britain's shipping. More than 20 cargo vessels were sunk in November 1940 alone;

RUTHLESS... AND RISKY

BY OCTOBER 1940, WITH the intricacies of Naval Enigma defeating even geniuses like Twinn and Turing, a more direct approach was needed. The obvious answer was to get hold of the hardware – a functioning Enigma codemaking machine. But how? The Germans would not simply hand one over. Any engagements between the two sides at sea were (naturally) unfriendly and, if successful for the British, ended with the German vessel at the bottom of the sea.

As Naval Intelligence pondered the problem, Lieutenant Commander Ian Fleming (1908–64) came up with the kind of scheme that, it's become conventional to say, might have come out of one of his later James Bond novels. In truth, it might have struck the reader as being improbably crude and gory.

'1. Obtain from Air Ministry an air-worthy German bomber,' his jotted outline for the plot began, before continuing: '2. Pick a pilot, W/T [wireless telegraph] operator and word-perfect German speaker. Dress them in German Air Force uniform, add blood and bandages to suit.' The next step, he said, was simply to '3. Crash plane in the Channel after making SOS to rescue service in P/L [plain language].'

After that, it would simply be a matter of the agents shooting their Samaritans, tossing their bodies overboard, taking over their vessel and sailing it back to Britain. To optimize their chances of being 'rescued' by the kind of sizeable and significant craft likely to carry the requisite coding equipment, Fleming argued, the 'crash' would best be staged well out at sea.

33 in December – despite the difficulties of fighting far out at sea in the storms and darkness of deep winter, which would normally have meant a lull in this kind of warfare. There was good reason for this convention. While January 1941 saw more than 120,000 tons of British shipping sent to the bottom by the U-boats, Dönitz was not in a festive mood. If the British had barely laid a glove on his fleet, the waves and weather had, and an uncomfortable number of his U-boats had to be brought in for repair.

Those left serviceable still accounted for a further 35 British ships in February 1941, though; in March, the British lost 243,000 tons of shipping. With his gift for phrasemaking, Churchill in a directive of 6 March gave this grim attrition the title: the 'Battle of the Atlantic'.

It happened that a Heinkel He 111 had not long since been forced down over North Berwick in East Lothian, Scotland. With some misgivings, Fleming's plan was authorized. In the event, it came to an anticlimactic end, with Operation Ruthless becoming 'Operation Useless' as the weeks went by and British spotter planes cruised the Channel without finding a suitable German vessel to stage a crash nearby.

Turing and Twinn were, apparently, massively disappointed by this failure, a superior observed. They came to him 'like undertakers cheated of a nice corpse'. Evidence that, despite what might seem an 'ivory tower' existence out at Bletchley Park, they knew that they were involved in a shooting, killing war.

Right: The flamboyantly imaginative Ian Fleming.

Above: Under attack herself, but refusing to go quietly, the *Bismarck* gives HMS *Prince of Wales* a severe mauling with her main guns.

for the 1418 men on board, only three of whom were saved. The *Prince of Wales* was also badly damaged, adding to a dismal day for the British.

However, the *Bismarck* had not made it through unscathed. She'd been caught by at least one shell and was shedding oil. She was forced to make for France for repairs, but by a roundabout route, since she would have to try to make a rendezvous with a supply ship out at sea to top up her fuel. So she limped along with – it must have seemed to her frantic captain and crew – half the Royal Navy on her tail. Planes from the aircraft carrier HMS *Victorious* slowed her further, managing to hit her with a couple of torpedoes. Despite the *Bismarck's* stricken state, the pursuing pack lost her for a while far out in the Atlantic amid confusion as to where she was headed and hence what her course might be.

BLETCHLEY AND THE *BISMARCK*

Bletchley Park entered at this point to play a small but arguably decisive part in the drama by intercepting a seemingly inconsequential message from a Luftwaffe officer far away in Greece. His son was serving on the *Bismarck* and he bent the rules by sending a coded message to him, asking where the battleship was headed. The reply of 'Brest' was enough to let

British warships and planes from the aircraft carrier *Ark Royal* to close with the *Bismarck* and start pounding her anew.

Throughout the evening of 26 May and the following night, the destroyers HMS *Cossack*, *Sikh*, *Maori* and *Zulu*, along with the Free-Polish destroyer *Piorun*, harried her relentlessly with torpedoes. Even now, she was struggling on, but her steering gear was badly damaged and her captain was forced to give up on getting to Brest and safety.

On Tuesday 27 May, the heavy cruiser HMS *Norfolk*, the cruiser the *Dorsetshire* and the battleships *King George V* and *Rodney* cornered the *Bismarck* and clustered around her in something of a feeding frenzy, pounding away with shells from just a mile or so away. Even so, it seems possible that it was *Bismarck's* own commander, Admiral Günther Lütjens (1889–1941), who delivered the coup de grâce: when the wreck was discovered decades later, it was found that she had been scuttled. Of the 2200 men on board, only 110 survived to be captured; the rest went to the bottom with their ship.

Below: Only 110 survivors from the *Bismarck* were rescued – the Battle of the Atlantic claimed up to 70,000 lives all told.

A CORNER TURNED

It may have been a triumph, but the *Bismarck's* sinking had to be set against a total of 510,000 tons of British shipping lost in May 1941, more than half of which (325,500 tons) had been dispatched by Dönitz's U-boat packs. The codebreakers were about to turn a corner, however. By the beginning of June, Bletchley Park had six bombes up and running, one of them dedicated solely to Naval codes. They could, suggests historian Hugh Sebag-Montefiore, read Enigma messages 'almost as quickly as the Germans'.

The new information paid off, quickly and handsomely. Partly out of caution and partly out of calculation, the decision was taken to use the decrypted intelligence in the first instance to attack Germany's supply ships rather than directly attacking the U-boats and surface warships they were serving. Between 3 and

STORMY WEATHER

IT MAY HAVE LACKED the cloak-and-dagger of Operation Ruthless or the spectacular heroics of the hunt for the *Bismarck*, but the capture of the *Lauenberg* was more important than it might seem. The idea had been that of Harry Hinsley (1918–98), a student of history at Cambridge before the war but at Bletchley Park a sort of 'meta-codebreaker'. He'd studied the flow of signal traffic, the rhythms and patterns it followed and the kinds of call signs and message structures used to glean insights into the size and shape of the *Kriegsmarine* and how exactly it was run.

This was all extremely abstruse by comparison with his realization in late April 1941 that Germany's weather trawlers used the same codes as their naval sister-ships but were essentially unprotected. At the end of May, accordingly, the *München* was stopped in waters northeast of Iceland and captured with its codebooks aboard. Another weather ship, the *Lauenberg*, was boarded on 28 June, again off Iceland. Its capture

Above: RAF Eastcote, Middlesex, became an outstation for Bletchley: over 100 bombes were operated here.

was carefully timed so as to allow the next month's Enigma settings to be seized.

Of course, in all things ULTRA-related, every silver lining came with its accompanying cloud. How long could it be before the enemy worked out that its weather ships were being deliberately targeted? How long after that before they realized why?

Left: A back-of-the-tapestry take on a modern engineering marvel. Behind the Bombe was a veritable rat's-nest of wires and plugs.

21 June, eight such vessels were ambushed and sunk, six of them on the basis of ULTRA information.

That was not the only dividend. In the first three weeks of June, not a single convoy was intercepted by U-boats: ULTRA information allowed their courses to be set so as to give the wolf packs a wide berth. This was an extraordinary achievement, but, to put it in perspective, U-boats and Italian submarines still succeeded in sinking 310,000 tons of shipping through the month as a whole.

The U-boats suffered similar dry spells in July, although again they managed an impressive number and scale of sinkings in between. That month, 120,000 tons of British shipping was lost to Axis actions; three-quarters of that tonnage was sunk by submarines. August brought a breakthrough: the 41 ships that were sunk represented a total of less than 100,000 tons for the first time in well over a year. In November, U-boats accounted for only around 62,000 tons.

A MATTER OF COURSE

The kind of contribution Bletchley Park was making at this time is well-illustrated by the story of Convoy HX 133. The HX

Above: One of many hundreds of merchant ships dispatched by the U-boats takes its crew and cargo to the bottom of the sea.

denoted its port of origin: Halifax, Nova Scotia; the number that it was the 133rd Atlantic convoy to set out from there. It did so, bound for Liverpool, on 16 June 1941: some 57 merchant ships, escorted by British and Canadian destroyers, corvettes, minesweepers ... seven warships plus a few armed trawlers. Arcing north and east along the great circle route which would take them towards Greenland and Iceland before bringing them southward and into the Irish Sea, they quickly fell foul of fog – and there were a number of collisions within the convoy.

But the real danger waited beneath the water's surface, where *U-203* was lurking. The convoy sighted, skipper *Kapitänleutnant* Rolf Mützenberg (1913–42) signalled Dönitz back in Brest to tell him so. Fortunately, his message was intercepted and successfully read by the codebreakers at Bletchley Park. So, too, was his fleet commander's alert to other U-boats in the area, who had duly started gathering for the kill. Bletchley Park's warning allowed the British Admiralty to let HX 133's escort know that they were being stalked and the wolf pack closing.

The convoy was immediately ordered to change its course. Escorts were taken from other nearby convoys which intercept evidence (or, rather, the absence of any) suggested weren't under any threat.

No miracle was worked. The convoy was still attacked – though its sudden switch of course had taken it away from where most of the U-boats had been heading. HX 133's escorts were ready, moreover, to mount the best possible defence. The U-boats ended up persecuting the convoy for five whole days – an anxious time for the Allied crews, no doubt, but an extremely frustrating one for Dönitz and his captains, who were investing considerable amounts of time, effort and risk without a result.

The arrival of the planes of Coastal Command finally tipped the odds against them too heavily for the U-boats' liking and this undignified skirmish finally petered out. By that time, six Allied merchant vessels had been sunk (albeit without any loss of life) but so had a couple of U-boats. Both sides by now were playing a numbers game, of course. Whilst the Allies could be pleased that 51 ships had made it safely to the Mersey, Dönitz was left to rue the loss of two more experienced skippers and their crews. For Bletchley Park, it was another job well done.

ADMIRALTY INDISCRETIONS

The calculus of success for Bletchley Park can seem almost as complex as its codebreaking work: the more the benefits, the greater the potential risks. The good run of the previous few months might easily have jeopardized the entire programme. As sparing as Churchill and his leadership were trying to be in applying their ULTRA information, it would

Below: The introduction of the large Type IX, with its longer range of 24,000 km (15,000 miles), allowed Dönitz to cast his net more widely.

always seem perverse to have such material and then not use it.

Hugh Sebag-Montefiore suggests it was just as well that this very summer the Germans had introduced refinements to their coding that would set Bletchley Park back again. Greater restraint was effectively imposed on the decision-makers by the fact that, after seemingly carrying all before them, the codebreakers were once more flailing in their work. While, as in the run-up to Cape Matapan, care had been taken to account for 'accidental' finds by sending out scouting aircraft to 'stumble upon' their targets, the aggregate totals had started to look too good to be true.

> IT WAS TO BE EXPECTED THAT, AFTER MONTHS OF PERSECUTION, THE BRITISH WOULD BECOME BETTER IN ANTICIPATING LIKELY HOTSPOTS FOR U-BOAT ACTIVITY.

Granted, it was to be expected that, after months of persecution, the British would become more canny in anticipating likely hotspots for U-boat activity and consequently in plotting convoy courses and in organizing countermeasures. Even so, it was difficult to avoid the suspicion that some more serious security breach might have occurred – how else to explain so rapid and so vast a change?

Dönitz is known to have been feeling wrong-footed and to have been pondering the reasons for this. The Germans did, however, set great store by the robustness of their codes, and suspicions seem to have been directed towards the possibility of old-fashioned espionage. The Admiralty did nothing to damp these suspicions down by the enthusiasm with which they began to apply some of the ULTRA information they were receiving.

The capture of *U-570* in the Atlantic on 27 August raised further suspicions among the German leadership. The U-boat's crew managed to destroy most of the relevant information on board before they abandoned ship. The Germans didn't know that, though, so naturally they wondered. They wondered more two months later, when the supply ship *Atlantis* was sunk by HMS *Devonshire* in mid-ocean: the British cruiser had appeared apparently out of nowhere. Just over a week later, the supply ship that had rescued *Atlantis*' crew, the *Python*, was sunk in its turn. Could this really have been coincidental? B-Dienst was now

Opposite: The capture of *U-570*, though in itself a coup for the Royal Navy, jeopardized codebreaking operations by putting the *Kriegsmarine* on alert.

AT THE CODE FACE

IT IS ONE THING to be bright and educated; another to be at home with the computational and cryptoanalytical ins and outs of what was being done daily at Bletchley Park. Welshwoman Mair Russell-Jones (1917–2013), then Mair Eluned Thomas, had not long graduated in music and German when she went to work at the Government Code and Cypher School. She didn't find it easy:

'I wasn't a mathematician and neither were the other women I worked with. I had never seen this kind of technology before, and even though it was explained to us several times how it all worked, it all sounded like double Dutch to me. And the atmosphere in our room, in fact in the whole hut, was silent. Sometimes the concentration was so dense you felt you were in treacle. We felt under pressure all the time.

'I'd sit there at the start of a shift feeling helpless and inadequate, not emotions with which I was particularly familiar. Until coming to BP I had known quite a lot of success, but Hut 6 disorientated me. Believe you me, when you're looking for the unknown using a machine you don't understand, it does nothing for your self-esteem.

'I know it sounds terrible and unpatriotic, but the work could be numbingly tedious. The menus were on large sheets of paper and full of lines and letters…

'The pressure was so intense that there was no pleasure in it. The process of keying in codes was time-consuming in itself, and then you had to try to decipher it. Sometimes I would stare and stare at this jumble, trying to make head or tail of it all.'

furiously combing all the British messages it had decrypted for clues as to whether the British might have decrypted theirs.

They seem to have decided that their system remained secure. Even so, Dönitz seems to have remained uneasy. He need not have worried so much, perhaps: despite all these successes, Bletchley Park was struggling to cope with the sheer quantity of material it was being sent. This was the context for that October's visit from Winston Churchill, which he hoped would boost morale, and for the subsequent letter from key codebreakers to the Prime Minister. The whole operation needed to be scaled up, they believed.

AMERICAN INTEREST

Attention was now returning to the Atlantic. The U-boats were beginning to up their totals again, but were also sowing confusion in other ways. A total of 80,300 tons of shipping sunk for August was by no means bad by recent standards, but the beginning of September brought more troubling news for the Germans. *U-652*'s attack on the USS *Greer* in a US 'security zone' southwest of Iceland may have been genuinely mistaken (she was under attack by RAF bombers at the time and her crew assumed the American destroyer in the background was British too).

The attack – with two torpedoes – may have been easily dealt with by the *Greer*'s crew, with no harm done. But President Franklin D. Roosevelt (1882–1945) was known to feel that the United States should be supporting the Allies more actively, and this incident risked giving him his *casus belli*. In the meantime, he settled for getting Congress to agree to altering the terms of the Neutrality Act to allow US ships to help in escorting convoys.

Below: The USS *Greer* fires depth charges: an inadvertent attack on this destroyer had helped precipitate America's involvement in the war.

Some 24 US vessels became involved in duties of this kind. There was a clear American interest in allowing this. But there was also a clear American stake in the war when, on 31 October, the USS *Reuben James* was sunk by *U-552* while on convoy duty. Over a hundred of the destroyer's crew were killed.

Even then, the United States stopped short of formally entering the conflict. The fact remains that, although the

IN THEIR OWN WORDS

To read the actual transcripts of messages decrypted by Bletchley's codebreakers is frequently to marvel at how much use was made of so little. That U-boat skippers didn't waste words is no surprise. Not only were they generally by their very disposition men of action: they wanted to keep their communications to a minimum in both frequency and length. Not so much from the fear of being decrypted as from concern not to spend too much time on the surface sending out transmissions.

'U 69 REPORTS NO CONTACT WITH THE CONVOY', reads one typical intercept; 'ENEMY IN SIGHT,' reports another, more excitingly. 'AM MAINTAINING CONTACT', another reassures Dönitz and Lorient. More ominously, the commander of *U-461* reports to headquarters that 'AM BEING SHADOWED BY 2 ENEMY A/C' ('aircraft').

Less obviously 'interesting' content could of course be invaluable to those in the Admiralty who were equipped to interpret it. Not least the location reported with each

message – and the point of origin detected by the intercepting Y-station on shore (given navigational errors or equipment inadequacies, the two didn't necessarily tally as they should). Frequently, too, there were observations on the amounts of fuel or air remaining, or on weapons malfunctioning or damage sustained – all this could help paint a fuller picture of what was going on.

Sometimes the messages hint at more poignant, personal stories, like this from *U-1221*, on 8 November, 1944: 'ORDINARY SEAMAN MOTYL WENT OVERBOARD IN NAVAL GRID SQUARE CC 1242 .... INQUIRY MAKES DESERTION SEEM PROBABLE.'

Dönitz, for his part, could be an exacting taskmaster. 'SEND SHADOWING REPORTS AT ONCE,' he scolds the skipper of *U-561*. On other occasions, he – or at least, his office – unbent. Enough, for example, to let Stoker Hampel on *U-608* know that 'DAUGHTER SIGRID HAS ARRIVED. HEARTY CONGRATULATIONS'.

Japanese attack on Pearl Harbor was still several weeks away, in the Atlantic the United States was already halfway to being at war.

After 7 December, of course, what had been a 'creep' to war became a full-on offensive. The surprise attack on the Pacific Fleet had made this just about inevitable. If, even now, war with Germany might have been avoided, that possibility was foreclosed when Hitler declared war on the United States on 11 December.

HAPPY AGAIN?

History has seen the United States' entry into the war as a pivotal moment. Rightly so: even allowing for the distraction of a war with Japan in the Pacific, the addition of America to the Alliance against the Germans would ultimately have a profound impact. In the shorter term, it gave the U-boats a new set of targets, naively crewed by men unseasoned in the Atlantic War.

Above: Waterproof-clad U-boat crewmen on a conning tower keep lookout for Allied shipping targets, some time in the summer of 1941.

Above: The commute between base and hunting-ground was costly in time and danger. Here U-boats resupply mid-ocean from a 'milch-cow' U-boat.

January 1942 saw the start of a second 'Happy Time' for the U-boat crews. Some 71 vessels – 327,500 tons of Allied shipping – were sunk by submarines; some 420,000 tons in all. There were easy pickings to be had just off America's eastern coast, where no blackout had yet been instituted.

Captain Reinhard Hardegen (1913–) of *U-123* brought his crew up on deck to see the show, he noted in his log, when the lights of Lower Manhattan came into view. 'Quite a bonfire we leave behind for the Yankees as a navigational help,' he added wryly after torpedoing the British cargo vessel *Coimbra* off Long Island. 'It's unbelievable,' he commented as, down the coast, he found passing tankers and freighters framed in silhouette by the glow from lighthouses, buoys and beacons, streetlamps, advertising displays and cars.

The Americans had been contributing escort vessels for British convoys for some time, but showed no sign of setting up

SECRECY AND SCALE

WHAT HAD ONCE PASSED muster as a 'shooting party' had grown rapidly in size. Ultimately, at the end of 1944, 9000 men and women would be working at Bletchley Park. Even by 1941, however, there were getting on for a thousand staff at the complex – expanded, as we've seen, by the addition of extra huts. Yet the need for secrecy was as great as ever.

The human resources problems with which Bletchley Park presented its managers could seem as intractable as any Axis code. How to add productivity without adding potential risk – if not of espionage, at least of indiscretion? If every worker was a potential blabbermouth, so was every security official or sentry. Who, as the saying goes, would guard the guards themselves?

And what of the all-important goal of cracking enemy codes? How was that to run smoothly if workers were mired in multiple levels of bureaucracy? Elaborate precautions had to be taken to keep the numbers with access to information to the absolute minimum while at the same time streamlining the efforts of those with the 'need to know'.

It would be an exaggeration to claim that these challenges were ever resolved. Like Britain, Bletchley Park did its best. That is no mean achievement, given circumstances in which, as the historian Chris Smith has commented, 'Even the morale-boosting act of providing a hard-pressed employee with a cup of tea became an extraordinary logistical and organizational feat.'

Above: A radio-intercept room at Bletchley Park today.

a convoy on their own account. The decision had been taken instead for US ships to hunt and destroy the U-boats themselves, wherever they were lurking. They were to find this a hiding to nothing. This early 'massacre' in the Atlantic may have played itself out over several months rather than a few hours and minutes, but it might be regarded as a sort of slow-motion Pearl Harbor for the Americans.

TAKING LIBERTIES

The British must have had mixed feelings. That US ships were being favoured over theirs can't have given much comfort; whatever weakened the Alliance was bad for Britain, that was clear. Then there was the paradox that the immediate impact of America's joining the war was an abrupt falling-off in certain sorts of aid. Since September 1941, for instance, US yards had been building 'Liberty Ships': basic cargo vessels put together from prefabricated sections and sent to Britain on a lend-lease basis. (Briefly, rather than demanding cash, the US took leases on the land for British bases while the conflict lasted.) The first one, *Patrick Henry*, launched in Baltimore on 27 September, had been completed by 30 December 1941.

By that time, however, American attention was firmly on the Pacific and the supply of new ships – desperately needed by the British – slowed. The effort would gather momentum over time: more than 200 'Liberty Ships' were built in 1943, and 2700 were constructed by the end of the war. For the moment, though, at a time when Britain felt its existence very much threatened, the looked-for support from the United States was not living up to expectations.

UP AGAINST IT

To add to Britain's problems, the codebreakers had been knocked sideways again by the introduction of a new and separate German naval code. Dönitz's concerns had not lessened as the months had gone by and, although there was still no clear evidence that the *Kriegsmarine*'s codes had been cracked, he erred on the side of caution. From February 1942, along

Opposite: Thrown together – though you'd never know it – the *Patrick Henry* slides down the slipway. 'Liberty Ships' helped save the British economy in the war.

Above: With four rotors squeezed in where three had been, the new-look Enigma made life disproportionately more difficult for Bletchley Park.

with 'Dolphin', there was another code: the more predatory-sounding 'Shark' (or 'Triton') just for the U-boat fleet – and just for the biggest single threat to Britain.

Also about this time, an extra rotor-wheel was added to the Enigma machine, meaning that four were squeezed in where there had been three before. This meant there were many more possible permutations, and consequently many more difficulties facing the Bletchley Park codebreakers. This coincided with a breakthrough by B-Dienst, who had made major inroads on Britain's naval codes. As soon as Bletchley Park had resolved one problem, a new one reared up to overwhelm it.

Meanwhile, the carnage at sea continued: that month, the U-boats accounted for more than 450,000 tons of Allied shipping, of which 679,500 were sent to the bottom overall. Bletchley Park's struggles were not just costing codebreakers sleepless nights: they were costing much-needed supplies – and, of course, seafarers' lives.

SCHARNHORST SHAMBLES

One of Bletchley Park's few triumphs from this time was the decryption of the news that the great battleship *Scharnhorst*, then in port in Brest, was going to head north to return to Germany. Ships and patrol boats in the Channel, and Luftwaffe bases on shore in France, had been placed on high alert ready to lend her their support as she headed through the Straits of Dover.

Scharnhorst had been recalled to play a leading role in the defence of Norway. That country was back in the strategic spotlight. Barbarossa hadn't been the clean sweep that Hitler had envisaged and he (rightly) feared that Allied supplies would get through around the Northern Cape. More extravagantly, he anticipated an Allied invasion of Norway to secure this route.

On 11 February, the *Scharnhorst* put out of Brest with two other warships, the *Gneisenau* and *Prinz Eugen,* and headed north and east into the Channel. Further ships sailed down from the North Sea to extend their protection. This was exactly as Bletchley Park had predicted, but the Germans managed to bamboozle the RAF and Royal Navy by sending out scores of fighter planes to buzz British radar and running interference.

By the time they had composed themselves, scrambled their own fighters and begun a serious pursuit on the water, the initiative had been lost and the *Scharnhorst* was well ahead in her dash for safety. Some face-saving damage was caused by mines dropped by British planes a few months previously, but the mighty battleship still got through.

Below: The Germans' Channel dash of February 1942 left the RAF and Royal Navy trailing, the British authorities red-faced.

This was an utter fiasco, then. Fortunately, by the kind of irony that quickly becomes familiar to the student of ULTRA history, the disaster had a positive impact in one respect: it reassured the Germans that their codes weren't being read. Had the British been privy to their plans, they could not have mounted quite so inept an operation – or so the Germans reasoned.

NUMBERS GAME

The attrition out at sea continued: 834,000 tons lost (538,000 tons to U-boats and Italian submarines) in March 1942; 674,500 (431,500 sunk by submarines) in April. May's total came to 705,000 tons (607,000 to U-boats and Italian

Y-STATIONS

BLETCHLEY PARK DID NOT, for the most part, collect the communications it decrypted – though some interception facilities were established there. Most of its raw material came from a series of Y-Stations around the country (the 'Y' was a pun on 'WI', for 'Wireless Interception'). They were run, not only by the armed services – the RAF, the Royal Navy and the Army all maintaining their own – but also by the GPO (the General Post Office) and security agencies. The Marconi Company, though a commercial operation, worked closely with the government at this time: it too maintained some Y-Stations on their behalf. Add to all this a community of amateur radio 'hams' and there was a nationwide network of wireless signal-interception.

The Y-stations, frankly, weren't much to look at: Arkley View in Barnet, north of London, was both a Y-Station and a distribution centre for information from around the country. But it was basically a big suburban house. The U-Adcock system mostly used for direction-finding was not much more than a little hut with four slender poles around it, set up at each of the cardinal compass points. This was generally some distance from the main interceptor so as to avoid interference between the two.

The direction-finding function may sound secondary, but it was crucial – for the location of enemy planes, for instance. Information on the exact whereabouts of German U-boats was, of course, key to ULTRA's contribution to the Battle of the Atlantic. Some traffic came in completely unencrypted and could be taken down and analysed by agencies locally. Coded transcripts were sent by motorcycle courier to Bletchley Park – though by the end of the War they were being relayed by teleprinter.

submarines); June's to 834,000 (of which U-boats and Italian submarines claimed 700,000).

If the situation wasn't as bad as it might appear, that's because the U-boat fleet was suffering wear and tear too, while Allied losses were beginning to be made up by construction in the United States. Even so, things were fairly dismal. This would have been the perfect time for Bletchley Park to work some magic, but they had frustratingly little to show for their efforts as the months went by.

'CONSPICUOUS COURAGE'

A stroke of good fortune came that November, not with a brilliant insight or technical advance at Bletchley but through the efforts of a brave trio of British sailors. Operating in the eastern Mediterranean, a few miles off the coast of Palestine, the destroyer HMS *Petard* became aware of the presence of a U-boat

Above: Dönitz's dilemma: out at sea, his U-boat capability was slowly being whittled down. In their bases (like this, at Trondheim, Norway), they weren't having an impact on the war.

Above: Caught on the surface in mid-ocean, a U-boat is attacked by Sunderland flying-boats, August 1943.

and dropped depth charges. *U-559* burst up to the surface, but promptly started sinking again, having been badly damaged by the British ship's attack.

Even as its desperate crew scrambled for their lifeboats, having opened the main valves to scuttle their defeated vessel, three men from the *Petard* – Lieutenant Tony Fasson (1913–42), Able Seaman Colin Grazier (1920–42) and cook's assistant Tommy Brown (c. 1926–45) swam the 60m (200ft) or so to the stricken sub and climbed on board. Brown was only sixteen years old, having lied about his age to join the Navy in the first place.

Total power failure had left the interior of the craft in darkness. Despite this, and despite the rapidly rising water level within, Fasson and Grazier succeeded in recovering the Enigma machine and books of codes, quickly but carefully wrapping them up to waterproof them, then handing them out to the waiting Brown. Before they could get clear themselves, *U-559* abruptly sank beneath the waves, taking them to their deaths. Brown himself was sucked down as the submarine settled, but after a struggle made it back to the surface with an up-to-date Enigma machine and the current Shark codes. Fasson and Grazier were awarded the George Cross for their valour; Brown (who was technically a civilian) the George Medal.

HELP AT HAND?

Bletchley Park set straight to work with the items Fasson and Grazier had secured at such a tragic cost; by mid-December, the U-boat code had been broken once more.

The difference immediately registered in the figures for shipping losses. In November, a total of 807,500 tons had been lost; 729,000 tons of that sent down by U-boats; for December the respective figures were 349,000 and 262,000. This was a reduction of about two-thirds – although figures tended to dip in the midwinter months anyway, which generally didn't offer ideal conditions for naval warfare.

The figures still made dismal reading. In all, 5.6 million tons of Allied shipping had been sunk worldwide in 1942 – the vast majority of it British shipping in the Atlantic. 1943 would be better; not so much because more ULTRA information became available (although a great deal did) but because the Allies were better placed to use it effectively.

U-559 BURST UP TO THE SURFACE, BUT PROMPTLY STARTED SINKING AGAIN, HAVING BEEN BADLY DAMAGED BY THE BRITISH SHIP'S ATTACK.

Below: A stricken Allied merchant vessel starts to settle in the water as its crew begins preparations to abandon ship.

AIR MILES

One major problem for the Allies had been the so-called 'Atlantic Gap' – the mid-ocean area that could not be covered by air from either Britain or the United States. As of 1942, this extended over 480km (300 miles) across from east to west, and over 960km (600 miles) up and down – from south of Greenland to north of the Azores.

This empty space was pretty much the U-boats' playground. Planes like the Wellington bomber could cover 560km (350 miles); the Sunderland and Catalina flying boats 710 and 1060km (440 and 600 miles) respectively, but this was nowhere near enough to get them to the 'Gap' and back again. Work had been under way for some time to develop longer-range aircraft:

Below: A B-24 Liberator escorts a convoy, far out at sea. The plane's introduction shifted the balance in the Allies' favour.

THE STORY OF SC 127

ON 13 APRIL 1943, Convoy SC 127 left Halifax, Nova Scotia, at that point numbering 54 merchant ships. A further four joined the convoy as it passed the port of St John's, Newfoundland. A 'slow convoy' (hence the 'SC' designation), it could manage no more than seven knots, making it a sitting target for wolfpacks waiting along the way.

But the supplies it was bringing – everything from tanks to timber, from sugar to steel, and from fuel to phosphates – were going to be vital to Britain's continuing attempts to fight. Whilst most were going to be unloaded at Loch Ewe, a deep inlet on Scotland's northwest coast, some ships were headed for Glasgow, Belfast, Liverpool and even London.

On 18 April, Bletchley Park decrypted a signal from Admiral Dönitz to his fleet. Ironically, it asked the pack to maintain radio silence. Except for reports of tactical importance. 'A convoy headed northeast is expected,' the Admiral had told his captains. And now, of course, told Bletchley Park too. Agonizingly, on the 19th, Britain's cryptanalysts couldn't find a crib, so that day's coded messages went uncracked.

Normal service was quickly resumed though, with the result that on 22 April, the convoy was warned by the Admiralty to change its course abruptly to avoid the wolf pack 'Star' lurking in the middle of the Denmark Strait between Iceland and Greenland. The new course took the convoy well to the north, bringing new problems with floating pack-ice, and further diversions were needed on this account. Even so, the alert from Bletchley Park had saved the ships from far greaer dangers: on 1–2 May, they finally reached Britain, all unscathed.

the B-24 Liberator had a range of 3850km (2400 miles) and was already in service, albeit in very small numbers, and they were needed in the open vastness of the Pacific. As 1943 went on, though, the aircraft would start to have an impact in the Atlantic.

The figures for shipping losses in March 1943 seemed as depressing as ever from the Allied point of view: 693,000 tons lost; 627,000 (108 vessels) of it sunk by U-boats and Italian submarines. But fifteen U-boats had also been destroyed that month, eight of them from the air, reflecting a significant shift in the balance of threat over the Atlantic.

Above: Generals Henri Giraud (left) and Charles de Gaulle (second right) meet F.D. Roosevelt (second left) and Winston Churchill (right) at the Casablanca summit talks.

Opposite: Between May and August 1943, 98 new U-boats were commissioned – but 123 were lost in action. Each of those losses represented a trained crew perished or taken prisoner. By the end of 1943, the *Kriegsmarine* knew that the average U-boat was unlikely to survive for more than three or four patrols.

In May 1943, U-boats sank some 265,000 tons of shipping (out of 299,500 lost). In return, though, 38 U-boats had been sunk. This was out of a total of 91 in the Atlantic – an attrition rate not too far short of 50 per cent. Twenty-one of these submarines had been destroyed solely by air attack (though three had been sunk by carrier-borne aircraft); fifteen had been sunk solely by warships. The devastation did not end there: many U-boats were badly damaged and had to return to their home bases for repairs.

A CHANGE OF MOOD

There were other factors contributing to a general shift in outlook. On 13 January 1943, leaders of the Western Allies came together for the Casablanca Conference, agreeing that they would continue with the war until they got the enemy's 'unconditional surrender'. This was fighting talk, and it reflected a feeling that the advantage had shifted sufficiently for thoughts of truces and negotiated settlements not to be needed. Stalin didn't make it to Morocco, being kept at home by the still-raging Battle of Stalingrad, although Commander General Friedrich

Paulus' surrender on 2 February would only underline the wider feeling that things were no longer going Hitler's way.

May was quiet in the Atlantic. Hitler had ordered his U-boats east into the Mediterranean to help support the supplying of those German forces still hanging on grimly in North Africa. The confined conditions of the Mediterranean did not really play to the U-boats' strategic strengths, nor were they cut out to act as escorts for relief convoys. In June, back in the Atlantic, U-boats sank 95,000 tons out of a total of 124,000, but at a cost. Seventeen U-boats were sunk that month. Another 37 went down in July; 34 in the Atlantic, although they still sank a creditable 46 ships (252,000 tons).

Despite these losses, the U-boats had clearly been a success: even now they were sinking serious quantities of Allied shipping. But the attrition rate was hardly to be borne. October saw another 26 sunk, largely by Allied aircraft. A major replacement programme had already been ordered, and more than 200 would

March–September 1943

— Extent of air escort cover

☐ Major convoy routes

• Allied merchant ships sunk by U-boats

⌁ U-boats sunk

■ Territory under Allied control

■ Territory under Axis control

☐ Neutral territory

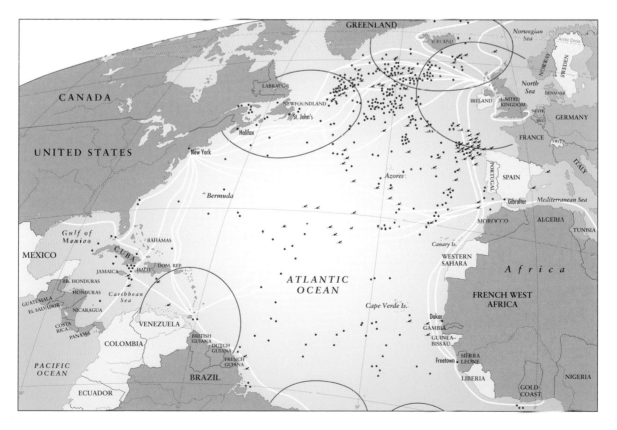

be coming into commission – but where would they find the required experienced captains and seasoned crews?

In any case, for how long would the Atlantic be as central as it had been? That July had seen the Allied invasion of Sicily, in Operation Husky. The Germans might have said (and truly believed) that the Italian surrender of 8 September was irrelevant, but it surely represented the writing on the wall. Turned back at Stalingrad in the east, ejected from Africa, and now forced on to the defensive in southern Europe, Germany had not yet been defeated, but it was hardly rampant.

ULTRA UNDER PRESSURE

Something of the same could be said of ULTRA – at this point in the war, at least. Later excitement about its 'war-winning' contribution would seem exaggerated on this showing. But then, no one was ever going to win a war by breaking codes. Alan Turing may have been the father of modern computing, but even he couldn't come up with a programme that could miraculously produce an Allied victory.

The workers at Bletchley Park – just like the soldiers in the desert or the crews of ships at sea – had to contend with the real-

Below: 12 June 1943: planes from the USS *Bogue* catch *U-118* on the surface. The attack ended with the U-boat's sinking.

'AN INSUPPORTABLE BLOW'

IN THE PACIFIC THEATRE, the Japanese seem to have remained supremely confident that their codes would resist any Allied attempts to understand them. They were certainly willing to commit remarkably full and detailed accounts of even the most sensitive plans, apparently sure that they would be safe. So it was that, on 13 April 1943, US interceptors picked up the following message from the office of Admiral Isoroku Yamamoto (1884–1943), one of the Imperial Navy's most experienced and charismatic commanders. The transcript was sent to FRUMEL (Fleet Radio Unit Melbourne, a sort of Anglo-American-Australian Bletchley Park) for decryption:

On 18 April commander-in-chief Combined Fleet will inspect Ballale, Shortland and Buin as follows: 1. Depart Rabaul 0600 in medium attack plane escorted by six fighters, arrive Ballale 0800. Depart at once in subchaser to arrive Shortland 0840. Depart Shortland 0945 in subchaser to arrive Ballale 1030. Depart Ballale by plane to arrive Buin at 1100. Lunch at Buin. Depart Buin 1400 by plane to arrive Rabaul 1540.

The Admiral was, it appeared, about to survey the state of readiness in a series of bases off Bougainville, with a view to a new offensive to be mounted in that area.

Not any more, he wasn't. Tipped off by FRUMEL, the US Army Air Corps had eighteen P-38 Lightnings airborne and ready on the appointed day. They ambushed the Admiral's flight just off Kahilin, near Buin, and after a brief dogfight his plane was shot down and he was killed.

'No one can replace Yamamoto,' said his successor, Admiral Minichei Koga: 'His loss is an unsupportable blow to us.'

world conditions they encountered. A young, inexperienced staff was essentially making up a new way of waging war as it went along. With brilliant minds on the Axis side constantly refining and developing their defences, they were invariably trying to hit a moving target.

If ULTRA had yet to win the war, it had repeatedly proven its value – if at times it had shown its fallibility, too. There were lessons to be learned about how Bletchley Park's energies and skills were best directed, and how its findings might best be incorporated into the Allied conduct of the war.

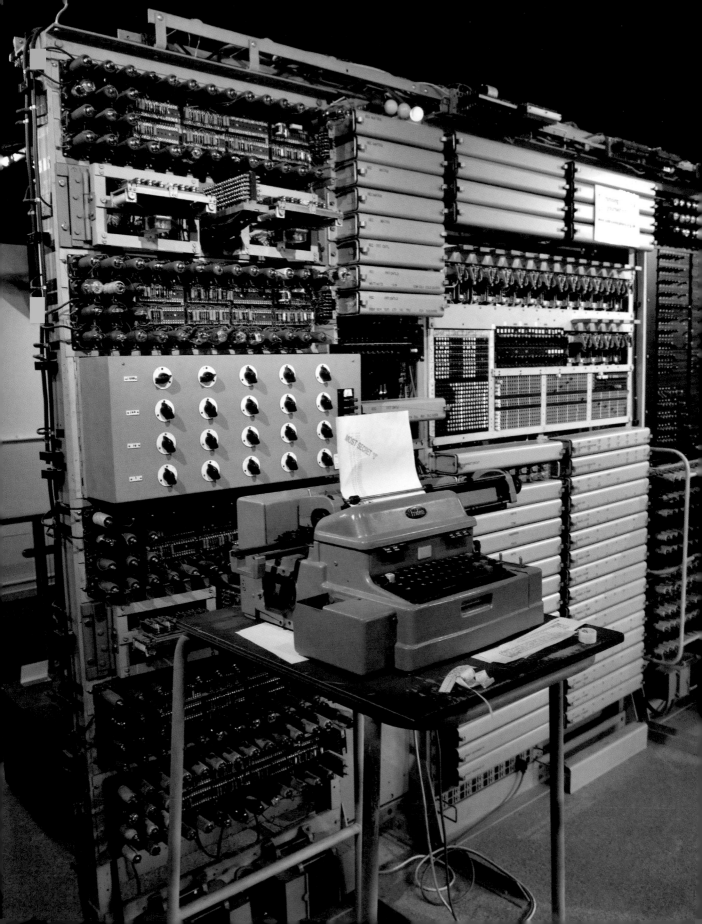

5

BLETCHLEY PARK 2.0

The Lorenz machine brought a new dimension of difficulty to what was already supremely challenging work. Bletchley Park's success in cracking these codes was an astonishing achievement.

F OR A FEW MONTHS in early 1944, a quiet stretch of coastline in Italy, south of Rome, became a lost corner of World War I. Here, as though preserved in amber, the Western Front was re-enacted, as if the last three decades had never been. The idea had been that a sudden landing here and a rapid advance inland would blindside the Germans and bypass their defences to the south. This would save weeks of delay, and any number of Allied lives. Instead, here they were, at a bloody standstill, mired in mud and pinned down by an inexorable bombardment.

Men who had dashed across the desert in pursuit of Rommel now hunkered in holes, cowering like rats in dugouts and ditches. 'The shriek of the shells flashing overhead, the fury of the explosions nearby and the terrible cry of the wounded men were nerve-searing beyond imagination,' recalled Edward Grace (1914–2011) of the 6th Battalion Gordon Highlanders. 'Our waterlogged trenches became more unpleasant every day.

Opposite: 'Colossus' by name, this reconstruction is colossal in size by the standards of the smartphone age – though its computational power would seem pitiful today.

Above: General John P.
Lucas let the Germans
take too much initiative
at Anzio. Luckily, Lorenz
had kept the Allies posted
on their plans.

Opposite: American
troops take cover in a
trench at Anzio, 1944.
Lucas' caution had meant
any advantage of surprise
being quickly lost.

It had now become a war of attrition
and endurance.'

TIME WARP

Perhaps fortunately for the Allied
troops, they were up against a foe
for whom, in important ways, the
last three decades hadn't happened
either. Field Marshal Albert
Kesselring (1885–1960) and Colonel
General Eberhard von Mackensen
(1889–1969) were consummate
professionals, modern soldiers
schooled in every development that
had taken place in the field of war.
Despite appearances, though, they
weren't really the ones in charge of
the German army defending Anzio.

Although their *Führer* had in other respects come a long way
since, as *Schütze* (Private) Hitler, he had served with the 1st
Company of the 16th Bavarian Reserve Regiment at Ypres
and Arras, his view of military tactics was still as it had been
formed there.

Kesselring's aim was, essentially, to sit back and defend
in depth, slowing the invaders' advance to Rome as much as
possible. Time was not on their side, he reasoned. He could
hardly believe his luck when, instead of driving straight inland,
the Allied commander, America's General John P. Lucas (1890–
1949), settled down and started consolidating his position on the
coast. The German Field Marshal came to share Churchill's view
that Lucas was fatally – and maybe culpably – over-cautious.
Given the strength of his own position, and the comparative
inexperience of many of his men, Kesselring thought it best to
hold his ground and let Lucas' passivity defeat itself.

However, Hitler did not want an army of his adopting so
seemingly passive a posture. Historians have frequently noted
the *Führer*'s almost pathological unwillingness to see his forces

give up an inch of ground for any reason. This probably had its origin in some strange, dark corner of his psyche. But the tactical philosophy that rationalized his obduracy here (as it had the previous year, at Stalingrad) was one he had come by in the trenches of World War I. Despite his supposed espousal of a high-speed, high-impact *blitzkrieg* theory, his instinct was always to see fighting as a shoving match over relatively small areas of territory. Military prowess was about being able to slug it out.

> THE NEW INFORMATION DID NOT WEAKEN THE ATTACK, BUT IT GAVE A HARD-PRESSED ALLIED FORCE ADVANCE NOTICE, AND AN OPPORTUNITY TO PREPARE.

Kesselring, then, was to concentrate his forces into the tightest possible front and advance aggressively upon the Allied army, in the German way. This could only lead to great and unnecessary loss of life, the Field Marshal knew, but he dared not disobey.

FORWARD-LOOKING

If Anzio had taken the Allies back into the past, what saved them came straight out of the future. Bletchley Park was way ahead of its technological time by now. More ingenious and efficient coding methods had called for more sophisticated responses, and British cryptographers were closing in on the Germans' most secure codes. In their quest for greater 'crunching' capacity, moreover, they were moving on from electro-mechanical to digital technology – to what was arguably to be the world's first true computer.

'Colossus', as it was to be called, was still some way off. Nevertheless, astonishing progress had been made. Along with its everyday Enigma traffic, Bletchley Park was now routinely reading the communications between the German military elite, including those between Hitler's office and Kesselring in Italy. Such messages made it clear that the German Field Marshal was under pressure to push forward and revealed the direction, date, time and strength of his counterattack. They also supplied the wider context, giving the Allied commanders a more or less complete picture of the strength and order of Germany's divisions in Italy at the time.

FOREWARNED, FOREARMED

The new information did not weaken that attack, but it gave a hard-pressed Allied force advance notice, and an opportunity to prepare. In the slightly longer term, it gave Allied command a broader perspective on things, with all the freedom of planning and of action that this brought. As Harry Hinsley would say:

It enabled them not only to pin down a million battle-experienced German troops with a minimum effort but also to reduce that effort without sacrificing that objective as they prepared for the landings in France.

To put it another way, it let them look up from their army's immediate predicament at Anzio and see a much more promising strategic situation. That the advantage brought by Lucas'

Below: Lieutenant General Mark W. Clark does what he did best, his critics charged: enjoying a photo opportunity as passenger in his jeep.

successful defence was to a considerable extent squandered by the impetuosity of his American comrade, Lieutenant General Mark W. Clark (1896–1984), is a reminder that the most advanced intelligence-gathering and the most sophisticated codebreaking techniques are no substitute for common sense on the ground. Overall, Anzio was chalked up as an Allied 'win'. It was in no small measure a win for Bletchley Park as well.

GONE FISHING

Since August 1941, work had been taking place on codes created by Germany's Lorenz machines – work that was just about coming to fruition now. Almost two and a half years was a lengthy lead-time, despite the work being carried out in the utmost haste. What is really extraordinary, however, is that the workers didn't give up at the outset, when they first appreciated the difficulties involved, and that they persevered as long as they did to attain a successful outcome. Research was conducted in tandem with work on the Enigma codes because the Germans

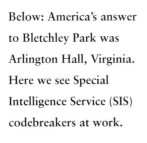

Below: America's answer to Bletchley Park was Arlington Hall, Virginia. Here we see Special Intelligence Service (SIS) codebreakers at work.

A CONTESTED LEGACY

THE VARIOUS PARTICIPATING intelligence services performed spectacularly well across the Allied wartime alliance. However, they did not always perform spectacularly well together. There were wheels within wheels and, almost, wars within the war. Co-operation proved anything but seamless. The loyalty that Commonwealth countries like Canada, Australia and New Zealand had for their British 'mother country' was tinged with sensitivity to being patronized. But any tension this feeling caused was as nothing to that between Britain and its former colony, the United States.

There were commonsensical reasons for the work of gathering intelligence on the Germans and the Japanese being divided between the big two Allied powers. Britain had already been fighting the Germans for some time when the United States joined the war, while America had taken up the main fight in the Pacific. There was more to it than this, though. However hard they worked to present a united front, there were real tensions between the two countries.

There were differences in 'corporate culture' too. British security services, which as late as the 1980s would attract ridicule for keeping secret the number of biscuits eaten weekly at their headquarters, were horrified at what they saw as informational incontinence on the US side.

News of several important early breakthroughs against the Japanese codes

Great box-office but an unforgivable affront to British heroes, said UK critics of *U-571*.

found their way into the US press – sometimes deliberately, it appeared. The US agencies insisted this had happened by accident, whereas Bletchley Park suspected it was to boost public morale in America.

The American authorities had good reason not to chase down those responsible for leaking one such breakthrough in the *Chicago Tribune* in June 1942: the fuss would have sent the story straight to Japanese intelligence, who, as it happens, missed the *Tribune*'s scoop.

Things would only worsen once the war was over and British agents had to bite their tongues as their American counterparts claimed credit for the breaking of the Enigma codes and for inroads on Japanese cryptography made at Bletchley Park and Melbourne. These claims were first made immediately after the war, but found a wider audience in 2000 with the release of the movie *U-571*.

DOWN ON THE FARM

THE FIRST Y-STATION SPECIFICALLY set up to intercept Fish traffic was established in 1943. State-of-the-technology it may have been, but it was built in the bucolic-sounding setting of Ivy Farm, Knockholt, not far from Sevenoaks. Today this is Kent commuter country, but at the time it was rural – the base had been a working farm till it was requisitioned. Now, reports one anonymous volunteer who worked here in the war, it was a top-secret installation, with 'wireless masts and barrage balloons surrounding the area and military guards at the entrance'.

Along with several dozen other young women, this volunteer did 'two or three weeks' of training in the local village hall behind the Three Horseshoes pub, 'learning to decipher tapes and codes into alphabetical letters'.

Then down to serious, grinding, boring work and very unaware of the vital importance of the job … in large, bare Nissen huts within the confines of the farm.

used them both at the same time. It had been clear from early on that certain high-status communications were written in codes that seemed unrelated to the (by now fairly familiar) Enigma output. Those who worked the Y-Stations had noticed that these transmissions made a very different sound to the radio signals the operators at Bletchley had been used to: they had referred to it as 'new music' at the time.

One reason for this difference was that these messages had been sent via teleprinter. This was a more complex system than the Enigma machine, which essentially reduced everything to an encrypted form of Morse. Teleprinters used a Baudot code (named for its French inventor, Émile Baudot (1845–1903)), which had 32 characters, allowing content to be handled more flexibly and as it were 'juggled', with multiple messages sent along a single wire at the same time. Taking a line through the German name for teleprinter communications – *sägefisch*, or 'sawfish' – British codebreakers had given this kind of traffic the nickname 'Fish'. The most often used they called 'tunny' – the word used then for tuna.

A MIRACULOUS MACHINE

The machine the Germans were using for their 'blue riband' messages was the Lorenz SZ42. It was expensive kit, which was why so few of the machines were used: in the region of 200, it's believed. In fact, no one at Bletchley Park would actually see a Lorenz machine until after the end of the war in 1945. Of all the challenges facing them, though, this was the least intimidating. Mathematical marvels that they were, they were happy enough carrying out their research and experimentation at a theoretical level, working back from the kinds of communications it transmitted to reconstruct the Lorenz machine imaginatively.

Designed to work with a regular teleprinter, encrypting messages, like Enigma, the Lorenz machine created codes by

Below: It seems absurd to say it but, given the complexity of the task it performed, the Lorenz SZ42 was wonderfully streamlined.

sequenced turns of revolving rotors. But it did so on an altogether grander scale, to an unimaginably greater level of complexity – so much so that the difference in degree amounted to a difference in kind.

By comparison with Enigma's three (or, latterly, four) rotors, the Lorenz machine had twelve, giving it 1.6 million billion possible start positions. Identifying one of these was like finding a single needle concealed in a line of several thousand haystacks. Worse than that: the use of unique 'one-time' encryption codes, randomly generated, placed an insurmountable perimeter around the field where the haystacks were.

In the event, this barrier was not the brick wall it seemed to be initially. That both receiving and transmitting machines had to have the same randomly selected one-time cipher was of course impossible to manage in a time of war. (How were sender and receiver supposed to be given the same random sequence to work with? If there had been secure communication there would have been no need for a code.) But the attempt to produce a machine that would generate a random sequence succeeded only in creating a pseudo-random one, which – however similar it might seem – was not the same thing; certainly not to the mathematicians at Bletchley Park, who were skilled in building out of the flimsiest of foundations.

Below: They don't look all that different, but the rotor wheels of the Lorenz machine offered many times the number of permutations Enigma did.

A STROKE OF LUCK – AND GENIUS

The breakthrough that came on 30 August 1941 originated in a stroke of sheer luck – although it was one that the codebreaker concerned, Colonel John Tiltman (1884–1982), had the talent and experience to take full advantage of.

HARD LABOUR

BILL TUTTE (1917–2002) HAD shown himself to be a brilliant mathematician at Cambridge, but was to surpass all those achievements at Bletchley Park. Working with John Tiltman, he undertook to decrypt the code in which 'Tunny' transmissions were taking place.

Although Tiltman's insight had been key to opening up the Fish codes in the first place, Tutte's intuitive skills were crucial to unpacking how the whole thing worked. It was he who discovered what became known as the 'statistical method', which, very basically, found that the Lorenz Codes concealed unseen probabilities in their apparent randomness.

Right: Bill Tutte is remembered in Newmarket, Suffolk, as a local boy.

Briefly, a German operator had sent a message – a decent chunk of text, 3976 characters long – that seemed impenetrable gobbledegook, as Tunny messages always were. However, apparently fearing that the first transmission hadn't succeeded, he had typed the whole thing out to send again. In his impatience, he had reused the original starting code – the sequence of letters that told the receiver where the rotors should be set so decryption could begin. He had also abbreviated some words this time round, and seemingly introduced some typos. Tiltman now had two copies of what was clearly the same text, coded with the same cipher, but with key differences that might afford him a way in.

The existence of these differences within what was simultaneously the same message gave the codebreaker an edge of perspective, a sense of depth. Rather than presenting a sheer and impenetrable surface gloss, the message now offered a sort of virtual three-dimensionality in which the cryptographer could find all-important leverage.

Above: A desk at Bletchley Park museum today, recreating the environment in which the code breakers worked. It looks a mess. But in the organized chaos of Bletchley, a new kind of creativity was emerging.

THE TESTERY

Following on from Tiltman and Tutte's discoveries, Bletchley Park management set up a new team jokingly referred to as the 'Testery', because it was led by Major Ralph Tester (1902–98). From 1 July 1942, he worked with Captain Jerry Roberts (1920–2014) and a few other cryptographers to apply Tutte's findings to actual German intercepts. Working entirely by hand, using methods that were as laborious as they were ingenious, the Testery succeeded in decrypting more than 500 messages over the following three months.

Their numbers boosted by additional staff, they could cope with more: over a thousand over the next three-month period. This represented an average of 15 messages a day – a figure that doubled in the first quarter of 1943. Typically, the more qualified codebreakers found those messages most likely to find a degree of 'depth', identified the wheel settings for that day's cipher, and were consequently able to come up with (slightly) simplified versions of the message.

After that, their junior staff were able to break these and other messages down still further, producing plain-text English versions of what were generally high-level communications. Although they would soon seem outdated, Tutte's techniques for hand decryption were indisputably effective: 90 per cent of the material that came to the Testery was successfully transcribed.

THE NEWMANRY

Another brilliant maths graduate, Max Newman (1897–1984) joined the Testery straight from Cambridge in the autumn of 1942, but quickly grew frustrated with the cumbersome business of hand decryption. As an academic, he had published important papers on pure mathematics and logic, but he'd also explored the idea of 'computability', imagining hypothetical computational machines. (He had discussed these to some extent with Alan Turing.) Chafing at the slow laboriousness of his daily work regime in the Testery, he had become convinced that more streamlined, mechanized systems might be devised. Impressed by his ideas, his superiors set him up with his own team – the 'Newmanry'.

WORKING ENTIRELY BY HAND, THE TESTERY SUCCEEDED IN DECRYPTING MORE THAN 500 MESSAGES OVER THE FOLLOWING THREE MONTHS.

Over the following few months, Newman worked with technicians at the Post Office Research Station in Dollis Hill, North London – most notably, perhaps, with Tommy Flowers (1905–98). He also had the bright idea of calling in Charles E. Wynn-Williams (1903–79), of whose recent work at Cambridge he'd heard talk. Wynn-Williams was a physicist, with no real

Left: Max Newman set about finding a way of mechanizing the work of the 'Testery': a significant step into the future for Bletchley Park.

experience of or interest in computational theory. However, the 'scale-of-two counter' that he had designed for counting atomic particles in nuclear physics turned out to be crucial for the construction of what its inventors would call the 'Heath Robinson' machine.

HEATH ROBINSON TO THE RESCUE

To this day in British English, the idea of the 'Heath Robinson' contraption exists: it can be any over-complicated and eccentrically conceived mechanical contrivance. It takes its name

DECODING KURSK

GENERAL FRIEDRICH PAULUS' SURRENDER at Stalingrad (on 31 January 1943) may have been the only reasonable course of action open to him, but Hitler's sense of its catastrophic significance wasn't wrong. As desirable as German domination of Western Europe might have been to him, his greater vision – the whole *Lebensraum*, Thousand-Year Reich thing – depended on his securing vast territories to the east. Now, having started off so promisingly, the invasion of the Soviet Union had at best been held; at worst, it was on the point of being thrown into reverse. The Germans had to get back on the front foot – and very soon.

Hence the humming of the wires from April onwards as plans for a new eastern offensive – 'Operation Citadel' – were drawn up and local commanders briefed on what their role would be. For such significant intelligence, the Lorenz machines were used. That the Germans' preparations were so thorough and so painstaking was

fortunate for a Testery team who as yet could not turn around their intercepted messages in anything like real time.

The Germans knew that they would face fierce resistance, as a dispatch from Field Marshal Maximilian von Weichs (25 April 1943) made clear:

In the event of 'Citadel', there are at present approximately 90 enemy formations west of the line Belgorod–Kursk–Maloarkhangelsk. The attack of the Army Group will encounter stubborn enemy resistance in a deeply echeloned and well developed main defence zone (with numerous dug in tanks, strong artillery and local reserves), the main effort of the defence being in the key sector Belgorod–Tamarovka.

In addition strong counter-attacks by strategic reserves from east and southeast are to be expected.

Thanks to the Lorenz decrypts, the Soviet leadership knew they knew this from the celebrated cartoonist William Heath Robinson (1872–1944), who pretty much created his own graphic genre, depicting humorous devices of this kind. Hence the name given to the first, faltering effort at mechanizing the decryption process for Tunny that was built at Bletchley Park during the early months of 1943.

By ideal, theoretical standards – and, for that matter, those of later computational practice – the 'Heath Robinson' was almost hopeless. Slow and temperamental, quicker in breaking down than in crunching codes, it would have driven a modern cryptographer mad. And it only provided half a

(although, as we've seen, they weren't – officially, at least – aware of the origin of this intelligence).

Nor did it stop there. Bletchley Park were able to give the Soviets detailed information almost three months in advance on the numbers of troops (800,000) and tanks (2500) and their likely dispositions in the weeks leading up to what was already envisaged as a giant pincer movement around Kursk. As a result, when the attack came on 5 July 1943, the Soviets were well reinforced and ready – first to resist the Germans, then to launch a counter-attack and force them into retreat.

Above: A column of German Tiger tanks prepare to enter the fray at Kursk. Thanks to the work at Bletchley, their numbers and positions were already known.

WHO'S WHO

THE EXCLUSIVITY OF THE **Lorenz messages** meant that those at Bletchley Park who got to read them got the sense of having a front-row seat on the unfolding events of World War II. Rommel's messages from North Africa crossed their desks; so did those of Chief of the Armed Forces High Command Field Marshal Wilhelm Keitel (1882–1946) and Chief of Operations of the Armed Forces High Command Alfred Jodl (1890–1946) and his deputy in Western Europe, General Walter Warlimont (1894–1976).

The direct danger to Britain itself apparently diminished, Bletchley Park had paid more attention to the Russian Front since the middle of 1942. Messages from Field Marshals Maximilian von Weichs (1881–1954) and Erich von Manstein (1887–1973) were read with enormous interest. Not until the beginning of 1944 would Lorenz yield up the 'scalp' of a

Field Marshal Wilhelm Keitel had few secrets from the staff at Bletchley Park.

message signed by 'Adolf. Hitler. Fuehrer.' – but from that time on there would be no looking back.

solution, producing the sort of simplified messages the qualified codebreakers had before: junior staff still had to complete the decryptions by hand.

Even so, it was a vast improvement on what had gone before: the business of painstakingly working out the basis of each code from first principles by hand already seemed to belong to some distant age. Between July and December 1943, with Heath Robinson up and running around the clock, the Newmanry was decrypting an average of 72 messages a day.

A COLOSSAL ACHIEVEMENT

The second half of 1943 saw Bletchley Park's computational
capacity transformed by the development of 'Colossus',
the world's first programmable computer. Although its
cryptanalytical logic was essentially the same as Heath
Robinson's, its technology represented a difference not just in
degree but in kind. In Heath Robinson, the message was input
and the decrypt produced by means of perforated paper tapes
that had to be kept completely synchronized at all times. This
was an electromechanical approach, reliant on the perfect
functioning of a significant number of moving parts; or, to put it
another way, a recipe for trouble.

The new machine developed by Tommy Flowers and his team
relied instead on an electronic analogue to Lorenz: the work
of one of the tapes was done by over a thousand thermionic
valves, switching on and off the current not electromechanically
but 'digitally'.

Below: Colossus's
control panel clearly
shows the paradox of the
coming technology: vast
computational power at
the operator's fingertips.

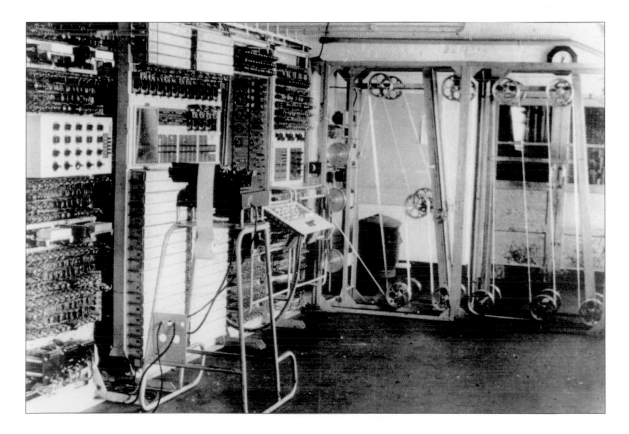

As with all things computational, great complexity grew out of great simplicity repeated over and over at fantastic speed. Colossus basically did what a human operative would have done, applying a method of trial and error, trying to read the input ciphered message against a succession of different imagined Lorenz wheel settings. But it did it far faster than any cryptographer could have dreamt of doing it by hand. From February 1944, with Colossus fully on-stream, Bletchley Park was handling 112 messages a day.

KESSELRING'S CURSE

Many of the messages with which Colossus was dealing had been sent to or from the office of Field Marshal Kesselring – codebreakers at Bletchley often read his communications before he did himself. His troubles at Anzio were just the beginning.

Below: An artificially-intelligent secretary: connected up with Colossus, this teletype terminal would ultimately print out the decrypted text.

In the months that followed, as he sought to conduct what his biographer Andrew Sangster has called an 'aggressive retreat' up the Italian peninsula in a succession of resolute but unavailing rearguard actions, Bletchley Park was to be the thorn in the flesh he didn't know he had. He never would know, dying in 1960 in ignorance of what a cruel hand military history had dealt him. ULTRA's secrets would not be revealed until more than a decade later.

But Bletchley Park was on the case when Kesselring signalled his readiness to retreat from Rome, and from that time on it was in on his decisions on a daily basis. Lest we be inclined to feel too much sympathy, it was also privy to his satisfied reports of villages burned and populations slaughtered in reprisal for attacks by 'guerrillas' – or, as they would now be characterized, pro-Allied partisans.

In any case, the existence of ULTRA information was no guarantee that Allied forces on the ground would use it – let alone that they would use it wisely or well. From the invasion of Sicily on, Sangster says, Kesselring was the beneficiary of blunders. All we can say in conclusion is that, on balance, Bletchley Park's contribution made things easier for the Allies, and more difficult for the Axis. In a conflict so vast – and, for much of its duration, so finely poised – as World War II, the smallest advantage could make an immense amount of difference.

Above: Good news – and not before time! But many years were yet to pass before Bletchley Park would have the recognition it deserved.

6

ENIGMA
ENDGAME

By the end of 1943, Bletchley Park was approaching full capacity, reading the most secret messages as a matter of routine. It was making an appreciable difference to the progress of the war.

'THE WORST JOURNEY in the world,' they called it, and Duncan Harris (1922–2014) did not disagree. He sailed on several of the Arctic convoys to Murmansk. He was the navigator/observer aboard a carrier-borne Fairey Swordfish torpedo plane – popularly referred to as the 'stringbag' because its cockpit was wide open to the Polar winds. Even so, the weather never really worried such a seasoned flier – hard as it could be finding a way back to the carrier through the mist and snow. It was the state of the seas that really shocked him, as he recalled many years later in an interview with Tatyana Movshevich of the *Moscow Times* (22 December 2013).

I never thought that a ship could do so many gyrations and convulsions. There was one moment when I was sure that we were going all the way over, as we rolled at least 45 degrees. The waves were absolutely terrific, and you saw these things coming towards you. I was not a sailor and to see it without navigational

Opposite: 'The eyes of the world are upon you,' General Eisenhower told his troops before D-Day. Fortunately, Bletchley Park had its ears on German communications.

*knowledge frightened the life out of me. Had we gone any
further, we would have fallen over, filled with water and sunk.
But luckily the ship rolled up and over.*

But the weather was not the most formidable of the threats
they faced: to an extent that would have surprised even veterans
of the Atlantic convoys, aid to the Soviet Union had to be (in the
words of one historian) 'fought through' to its destination every
time. Every vessel had to run the gauntlet of U-boats, battleships,
torpedo planes and bombers sent to bring about its destruction
by an enraged *Führer* who seems to have taken every bit of
British assistance to the Russians as a personal affront. Not only
were they Red revolutionaries, they were Slavs and therefore
untermenschen; the very survival of their state was an insult.

At Bletchley Park there were no such perils. The only
'gyrations and convulsions' taking place were in the
extraordinary minds starting to reimagine our technological

**Below: The Duchess of
Cornwall is introduced
to the complexities of
the Enigma machine by
wartime codebreaker
Eileen Johnson.**

DEATH OF DELILAH

BY MID-1943, ALAN TURING had moved on – if not to greater, than at least to different, things. He was now based just a few miles north of Bletchley at another old country house, Hanslope Park. This was the headquarters of the Radio Security Service, on whose behalf Turing would be working for the next while. 'Delilah' was a way of encrypting and decrypting the spoken voice for telephone transmission – and real progress was being made by the early months of 1944. A prototype system was tried out that June: a speech by Winston Churchill served as guinea pig. The test was a triumph – those stentorian tones were successfully scrambled so all an interception could pick up was raw white noise before being reassembled for its designated hearer at the other end. However, the system didn't work with wireless radio signals over any distance and, in any case, it was clear that the war was coming to its end. Delilah languished, undeveloped, with Turing's work on it largely wasted. Fortunately, he would have other discoveries to his name.

and cognitive relationships with the world. The work the codebreakers did as they wrestled with the Lorenz communications helped usher in what would eventually be hailed as the Information Age.

ENIGMA AS USUAL

Such rarefied research as the Delilah system was confined to a small minority. The bulk of Bletchley Park's decryption work was done on communications in those same Enigma codes that they had been cracking for several years now – and that were still the stuff of everyday communication for the Germans. Monitors of naval traffic didn't seem to be hearing much of the 'new music' that some of their colleagues had started to pick up in messages from the higher echelons of intelligence and army command. At sea, there was no real sign of 'Shark' or 'Dolphin' giving way to 'Tunny'.

As we've seen, in the course of 1943, the Allies had put increasing pressure on the U-boats in the Atlantic, largely

Above: There for the taking... The Allied Convoy *PQ 17*, as seen from a German reconnaissance plane, after its departure from Hvalfjord, Iceland.

thanks to the work of Bletchley Park. But the success of Enigma decryption here had, if anything, only helped to turn the screws on the Arctic convoys, since the wolf packs were increasingly concentrating their attentions there.

RUSSIAN ROULETTE

There was already quite a chequered history with Russia. The rigours of the route around the Northern Cape to Kola and the White Sea were challenging at the best, most peaceful, of times. Now each trip was a tragedy in waiting. In the summer of 1942, convoy *PQ 17* had been severely mauled, with 24 of its 35 merchant ships sunk. Convoys had been suspended in response to this catastrophe and would not resume until the autumn of that year. However hostile the Arctic storms, the cover of almost day-round darkness had started to seem preferable to the perma-daylight of the summer months.

In 1943, the convoys were suspended after the arrival of homebound Convoy *RA 53* in Loch Ewe on 14 March. Not until 1 November did the first vessels of *JW 54A* leave Liverpool to head up the Irish Sea and through the North Channel to Loch Ewe, where they were joined by several more. HMS *Onslow*, under the command of Captain J.A. McCoy (1900–55), headed a flotilla of seven destroyers as the convoy's escort.

SHIFTING PRIORITIES

THERE WAS NO SIGN as yet that what we now know as 'Information Technology' would reduce manning levels – quite the contrary. By the beginning of May 1943, 4000 people were working at Bletchley Park; that number would only increase as the months went by. This was a World War: the conflict never slept and neither could the codebreaking operation. A shift system had been introduced so that 24-hour coverage was assured: each day was divided into three eight-hour shifts.

Shift work is stressful. Many Bletchley Park employees suffered not only from everyday exhaustion but also from disrupted sleep patterns when at last they did go to bed. These difficulties contributed to a range of complaints from fatigue to fainting, from disturbing dreams to digestive problems. In the worst cases, men and women had to be excused from service or transferred to other fields. Such issues were experienced by shift workers in just about every area of the civilian economy during the war years. The one great dividend for the worker was that,

The future Baroness Trumpington, Jean Barker, worked in naval intelligence at Bletchley Park. She spent her weekends socialising in London.

at the end of a week of daily shifts, he or she could expect a day and a half off work. This was a decent chunk of time; long enough to make a trip to Luton or Dunstable by train. More adventurous souls would venture as far as London, where they could go to a restaurant, concert or film. For the serious student of culture, there was Stratford-upon-Avon, where one could see a Shakespeare play. Money might be short, but the nation's cooperative spirit was high: hitchhiking could hardly have been easier.

FLOATING TROPHIES

WINSTON CHURCHILL'S GREATNESS AS a leader may be arguable and as a historical chronicler questionable, but there is no doubt that he was the greatest phrasemaker of the war. Summing up the early dreadnoughts in the first volume (1923) of his history of World War I, *The World Crisis* (1923–31), he had described these redoubtable vessels as 'floating fortresses'.

We have already seen that these big beasts of naval warfare were not as impregnable as they had once appeared, but they still maintained immense military charisma. They might not be 'floating fortresses', but they were certainly floating talismans, possessing enormous glamour for the countries they represented.

For the enemy, conversely, they took on something of the status of floating trophies, their value well outstripping their strategic significance. Not that this significance was negligible, even now, given the awesome size and reach of their guns, but ships such as the *Tirpitz* and the *Scharnhorst* were symbolically potent as well. Their intimidating size and strength were only part of their appeal. Ever since, in February 1942, it had made its audacious escape up the Channel from Brest, the *Scharnhorst* had been an emblem of German seamanship, dash and daring.

Meanwhile, Bletchley Park had played its part in planning and preparing a series of attacks on the *Tirpitz*. Most recently, in Operation Source (September 1943), a team of divers sent in with X-class midget submarines and mines had attacked it in Norway's Kåfjord and inflicted some serious damage: up to now, however, this fortress too remained afloat.

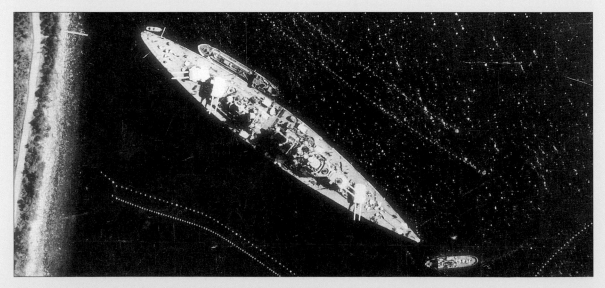

The *Tirpitz* 'before' – a threat but also a tempting target; hence the torpedo-nets hemming it in.

In the event, they would not be needed. To some extent, this
was a game of chance, and chance was on *JW 54A*'s side. Five
U-boats, half a dozen surface ships and many reconnaissance
aircraft were sent out to waylay the convoy as it made its way
around the northern tip of Norway and into the Barents Sea.
But they never found it, and the convoy reached Murmansk and
Severomorsk unscathed.

A 'Northern Task Force' – the battleship *Scharnhorst*, and
the five destroyers with it, waited in the shelter of the Altenfjord,
near the northern tip of Norway, for the call to action, which
in the absence of any contact, never came. The group as a
whole was under the command of the *Scharnhorst*'s master,
Konteradmiral (Rear Admiral) Erich Bey (1898–1943), a naval
officer since World War I.

The *Tirpitz* 'after', sunk
by Lancaster bombers of
the RAF, when a long and
varied series of previous
attacks had failed.

BAITING THE TRAP

Although resting quietly enough at anchor now, the *Scharnhorst*
still spooked Allied commanders: its presence represented a
continuing threat to the Arctic convoys. There was no reason
to assume that future ventures would share *JW 54A*'s good

Above: In 1946, Bruce
Fraser was to become
Baron Fraser of North
Cape: a career that had
taken him around the
world culminated here.

fortune. As long as the *Scharnhorst* remained holed up in the Altenfjord, however, Allied commanders would never know when it would reappear and play havoc with their shipping in the Barents Sea. The decision was accordingly made to set a trap to lure *Scharnhorst* from its lair: Convoy *JW 55B* would be the bait.

The convoy's 19 merchant ships left Loch Ewe on 20 December, its escort led by the Canadian destroyer, HMCS *Huron*. Several smaller vessels – corvettes and minesweepers – were in close attendance, while a number of destroyers provided distant cover. Further off again, but in constant touch, was a group commanded by the Home Fleet's Commander-in-Chief, Admiral Bruce Fraser (1888–1951), setting out from Iceland in support. Fraser's flagship was the battleship HMS *Duke of York*, but he also had a cruiser and a couple of destroyers. Also in the background was a cruiser group – Force 1 – under the command of Vice-Admiral Sir Robert Burnett (1887–1959). His flagship was the light cruiser, HMS *Belfast*; cruisers HMS *Norfolk* and *Sheffield* were there as well.

LAST CHANCE?

Fraser was convinced that, having missed Convoy *JW 54A* completely, the Germans would try twice as hard to stop *JW 55A* getting through. That November, Bletchley Park decrypted a communication that confirmed the admiral's conviction.

'The functions of the ships remain unaltered...' Naval Command had told its captains. 'Against this traffic', it went on, in clear reference to the continuing Arctic Convoys, 'both the Northern Task Force and the U-Boats are to be deployed.'

Interestingly, they seem to have been unaware that homebound Convoy *RA 55A* would be heading west from the White Sea at much the same time. The appearance of Convoy *JW 55A* promised good hunting in any case.

This wasn't just about taking prizes, though: every Allied convoy that got through to Russia would make the Soviet defence a little stronger. Not that it could really be called a 'defence' by now: since the surrender at Stalingrad and the failure of Operation Citadel, the Germans hardly had an offensive worthy of the name. Deep as they still were in Russian territory, they had lost nearly all the initiative they had once enjoyed and were holding on in mounting desperation while the Soviets increased in strength. When the moment came for a codename to be given to the Northern Task Force's latest sortie, the usual cryptic thinking was eschewed. The title Operation *Ostfront* ('Eastern Front') did not leave its deeper purpose to the imagination; it might as well have been called 'Eastern Front: Last Chance'.

READY FOR ACTION

A message sent on 18 December and decrypted by 20 December confirmed that the bait was being taken. The communication said that the Northern Task Force was ordered to take 'preparatory measures so that departure would be possible at any time'. The implicit message for Fraser and his fleet was equally clear: they also had to be ready to take action 'at any time'.

Enigma yielded yet more detail: that same day, Fraser was informed that the *Scharnhorst* had been placed

Below: Now a tourist attraction, tied up by Tower Bridge in London, HMS *Belfast* was in the thick of the fighting in the Arctic and elsewhere.

on three hours' readiness – although that notice was doubled to six hours on 21 December. Bletchley Park dropped the ball a little with the next message, placing the battleship on just one hour's notice for 25 December – this communication was not decrypted for some days. It didn't matter, however: on 24 December, the British admiral had heard that a patrol boat in the mouth of the Altenfjord had been warned that *Scharnhorst* would be passing at 1800 hours the following evening – that is, 25 December. Confirmation came in the early hours of 26 December from German sources – via Bletchley Park – that the battleship was now well out at sea.

Below: The big guns of the *Scharnhorst* face to offer a broadside. If a ship of this size and power caught up with an Allied convoy, it would cause mayhem.

RUNNING INTO TROUBLE

Fraser's signal to Convoy *JW 55A* and its close escort to swing to the north to avoid attack was intercepted by German monitors. Fortunately, it was their turn to drop the ball. They did not pass on the intercept, so the convoy's change of course went unnoticed while the *Scharnhorst* sailed on to where it 'should' have been. The British now had a second stroke of luck: although they were sighted by German spotter planes, who called in the presence of '5 warships, one apparently big', headed in the direction of the Northern Task Force, this warning too was missed until much later.

CONFIRMATION CAME IN THE EARLY HOURS OF 26 DECEMBER FROM GERMAN SOURCES THAT THE BATTLESHIP WAS NOW WELL OUT AT SEA.

The day was drawing on; Bey, having failed to find the Allied convoy where he'd expected to, assumed he had missed it and gave the order to come about. He sent off his destroyers to fan out separately so as to extend the search over a wider area. This was not as sensible a plan as it might have seemed: the *Scharnhorst* was now on its own and the southward course it was following was taking it straight towards Force 1, which was closing fast. They spotted the German warship shortly after 9 a.m. Shots were fired by Burnett's force from some 12km (7 miles).

Unsurprisingly at that range, not too much substantive structural damage was done to the *Scharnhorst*, although – by yet another stroke of luck – one shell disabled the battleship's radar system. The *Scharnhorst* circled to the northeast while Burnett's group gave chase. But engine trouble hampered HMS *Norfolk* and *Sheffield*, while HMS *Belfast* could not quite close.

CLOSING FOR THE KILL

With Fraser's *Duke of York* group drawing near and picking up the *Scharnhorst* on their radar, the whole situation was transformed. By 16.48 that afternoon, the *Duke of York* was within 12km (7 miles) of the German battleship – a comfortable enough distance given that HMS *Belfast* was closer still. Star shells from Burnett's light cruiser flooded the scene with light,

Above: A victory at sea was also a victory for morale at home. The sinking of the *Scharnhorst* gave Britain a great lift.

and the *Duke of York* had a fully illuminated target. A succession of salvos left the *Scharnhorst* badly damaged but still fully mobile as she beat a hasty retreat towards the east.

Now with several British ships in pursuit – not just the *Duke of York* with her guns but destroyers sending torpedoes after her retreating wake – the *Scharnhorst* had to twist and turn, and could not make rapid progress. As some of the torpedoes struck, on either side, the battleship was slowed still further. Closing quickly now, the *Belfast* once again lit her up with star shells, and the *Duke of York* opened up with her big guns. Her crew defended courageously and smartly, inflicting significant damage on the pursuing pack, but only one outcome was really possible now: the battleship went down at 19.45. Only 36 of the 1968 men on board were saved. The sinking of the *Scharnhorst* was a tragedy, but a great weight was taken off Allied commanders' minds.

CRUNCH TIME

The Allies now seemed to be closing in for the kill in the wider war. There was a sense of mounting expectation at Bletchley Park during the early months of 1944. 'We all knew that something was afoot,' Mair Russell-Jones would remember: 'but we didn't know what it was.'

What was afoot was Operation Overlord, the Normandy Landings and the Allies' eastward drive towards Berlin. 'The workload was now greater than ever,' recalled Russell-Jones.

None of us had any idea at the time that we must have been deciphering the Germans' plans for that part of northern Europe...

We weren't given any detailed information about the operations being planned, but we were told that this would be the greatest offensive attack launched by the British and Allied troops in Europe to date.

That was about the extent of the Germans' information, too: they could see that the Allies were going to make their move across the Channel or the North Sea and that it was going to be a major offensive, but they didn't know where the attack would come.

IRONIC ENTERTAINMENT

IN APRIL 1944, AS its contribution to the local community's efforts for 'United Aid to China' week, Bletchley Park employees put on their production of Patrick Hamilton's popular melodrama *Gas Light*. This had premiered to great acclaim in London's West End in 1938, although it was now more famous from the 1940 film, with Anton Walbrook and Diana Wynyard playing Jack Manningham and his wife, Bella.

Bletchley Park 'gas-lighted' the German command as surely as Anton Walbrook did Diana Wynyard.

Today, to 'gaslight' means to psychologically abuse a partner by chipping away at their confidence in their own perceptions and, consequently, their sense of their own sanity. The usage is familiar to thousands who have seen neither the play nor the film.

It is doubtful that the Nazi leadership would have known them either, although they certainly experienced something of what poor Bella did. Despite a couple of close shaves, the Germans never did discover that their codes were being read, although, as the months went by and the tide of the war turned against them, they were conscious of suffering some extraordinarily bad luck.

Rommel (under something of a cloud since he'd had to take the blame for defeat in North Africa, but still highly regarded for his professionalism) was called on to inspect the so-called 'Atlantic Wall'. This elaborate system of static built defences stretched from the southern shores of the Bay of Biscay to those of Norway. Rommel naturally focused on the central stretch, between the northern coast of France and the Netherlands.

ROMMEL'S REINFORCEMENTS

Below: Rommel, touring Normandy, visits the 21st Panzer Division – former comrades from North Africa. Here his scope for action was to be much more constrained.

Rommel's report on defensive preparations appears to have been lost, but as Arthur J. Levenson (1914–2007), an American cryptographer attached to Bletchley Park, who helped decrypt it recalled, the Field Marshal had not stinted in his report. It was, said Levenson, 'an enormous message':

I think it was 70,000 characters and we decrypted it as a small pamphlet. It was a report of the whole Western defenses.

ermann Harz

How wide the v-shaped trenches were to stop tanks, and how much barbed wire. Oh, it was everything and we decrypted that before D-Day.

The message may have been enormous, but its conclusions could hardly have been briefer. In Rommel's view, occupied Europe was extremely vulnerable. Although he is thought of as a swashbuckling desert general, Rommel showed his adaptability here by urging that static and constructed coastal defences be beefed up several hundredfold. He hoped to take some of the strain off what he felt were woefully ill equipped and poorly trained army units.

Thousands of new bunkers were built, and obstacles against gliders and paratroops raised, at Rommel's request. Of the 100

Above: Hitler's Atlantic Wall looked rather more impregnable than it really was. With ULTRA's help, the Allies were to find its weak-points.

million mines he asked for, only 5 million were to be laid in the
months that followed, but even this represented a considerable
reinforcement. From the Allied point of view, the great thing
was that – thanks to Rommel's punctiliousness – they had
detailed descriptions of what had been done
and where.

FROM THE ALLIED POINT OF
VIEW, THE GREAT THING WAS
THAT THEY HAD DETAILED
DESCRIPTIONS OF WHAT HAD BEEN
DONE AND WHERE.

DEFENSIVE DISPUTE

While infantry and artillery kept guard along
the Atlantic Wall, Rommel was to argue,
Germany's Army should be distributed along
the coast a little way inland. That way it
could do service as a mobile reserve force,
ready to come down with immediate support wherever any
landing should take place. But this view conflicted with that
of Rommel's superior on the ground, Field Marshal Gerd von
Rundstedt (1875–1953), Commander-in-Chief of the German
Army in the West.

Rundstedt was a distinguished general: his view that the
panzer forces should be kept back further inland, in fewer, larger
concentrations so as to be able to pack a greater punch in the
counterattack as the invaders assembled in open country was
logical enough on its own terms. Rommel believed this idea was
based on experience of the Eastern Front and underestimated the
logistical strengths of the Western Allies: they couldn't be allowed
even to approach the shores of continental Europe, he believed.

In the event, neither man would get his way: Hitler's
compromise solution – to give Rommel his 'line' of panzer
divisions (but in a slender, straggling, ineffectual form) and
Rundstedt his concentrations (but so small as to be useless) – left
both commanders anxious and frustrated.

Opposite: Gerhard von
Rundstedt outranked
Rommel but was to fare
no better in having his
opinion heard by Hitler.
Both were overruled on
Normandy's defence.

D-DAY DELIBERATIONS

Operation Overlord has generally been described in epic
terms: how else to describe the largest naval, air and
amphibious operation in history? It is also described in terms
of its human cost. After all, while so many were fighting and

Above: All the bustle of an English harbour... only crowded not with fishing boats but US landing craft, ready for the assault on Normandy.

dying on the beaches of Normandy, no one at Bletchley Park suffered so much as a scratch. That doesn't mean that the codebreakers didn't do their bit, of course, but it does make their contribution harder to assess. Some (not least Dwight D. Eisenhower) have suggested that the invasion of France could not have gone ahead without their backing, but it is hard to point to particular examples of heroics.

Much depends on perspective: the impact of a headline event like Operation Bodyguard simply isn't measurable. It is clear that it helped, not only, at first, as a tactical diversion, but also (when the ruse became clear) as a demoralizing, destabilizing feint, but it is more difficult to establish its significance. Ultimately, it is as decisive or as unimportant as we think it is. It seems fair to say that Bletchley Park's contribution was cumulative: a bit of information here, an insight there, but by now coming in a constant and ever-growing stream.

Bletchley Park's was a monitoring role, so essentially passive. In this time of mounting tension and accelerated decision-making, however, the information it picked up could be very quickly translated into action. Sometimes all that was necessary was for the effectiveness of existing strategy to be endorsed. So it was with the whimsically titled Operation Chattanooga Choo-Choo, in late May.

VIRTUAL REALITY

THE WORLD THAT BLETCHLEY Park was to usher in offers a wide range of alternative existences: some fanatics spend as much time gaming as they do in the 'real' world. Many focus as much on their 'Second Life' (a genuine online game) than they do on their first and supposedly real one, buying property, pursuing careers, having relationships; marrying, even. Most of us are familiar with the idea of the avatar – the Internet identity that is distinct (and maybe very different) from the real-life one.

Such a situation would have been unimaginable in the early 1940s, when most people in Europe would have felt that there was enough 'real' reality to go round. In hindsight, however, there might have been an early intimation of what was to come. Almost as much attention was lavished on the preparations for Operation Bodyguard as on Overlord – the Normandy invasion from which it was designed to distract attention. Hence the appearance of wood and canvas 'camps' along the English side of the Straits of Dover; the serried squadrons of mocked-up planes and lined-up landing craft. There was even a full-sized fake invasion headquarters set up at Dover, along with all the signals traffic needed to lend credibility to the deception.

In the meantime, British signallers kept up a constant stream of communications hinting at the likelihood of an attack upon the Pas de Calais, while bombing campaigns (twice as heavy here as in Normandy) helped boost that perception.

Thanks to Enigma decryptions, British double agents had much of the authenticating information that they needed to pass off disinformation as the real thing. Hence the elaborate preparations the Germans had to make in Norway to resist the (fictional) landing of Operation Fortitude North: 12 divisions were kept pinned down here.

Further attacks were hinted at in the Balkans and the south of France to keep the overstretched Germans on their toes. All the while, Bletchley Park was keeping track, taking the temperature of German responses, and making sure that the deception was succeeding.

Rommel certainly didn't see the funny side when more than 70 bridges and tunnels were destroyed in a series of raids targetting northern France's railway network. Depots, sidings and marshalling yards were also hit; messages decrypted at Bletchley Park showed that the Field Marshal was beside himself with anger at the disruption to troop movements and supplies. The shortage of spares was severely restricting his panzers' scope for action, he complained: tanks were being sidelined with what should have been minor problems.

In other cases, decrypts precipitated immediate and important changes of plan. News of the unexpected movement of the 91st Infantry to the Cotentin Peninsula, caught by quick codebreakers at Bletchley Park, prompted the cancellation of an earlier US decision to drop paratroops (the 101st Airborne) at La Haye-du-Puits.

Below: US DUKWs make their way ashore in Normandy. They encountered fierce resistance: without ULTRA information, though, the whole venture might have been impossible.

Left: Carefully coordinated bombing raids created havoc behind German lines in the run-up to D-Day, severely hampering Rommel and von Rundstedt's efforts to move troops to the Allied beachheads.

A WEATHER EYE

The main thing that monitoring indicated was continuing confusion on the German side: one decrypted Luftwaffe report anticipated an Allied landing near Dieppe. At the beginning of June, further decrypts in the days leading up to the planned invasion made it clear that the Germans had discounted the threat of an immediate attack. They calculated (reasonably enough) that four full days of good weather would be needed for a cross-channel landing, and did not expect such a window to occur for the time being. The loss of their Arctic weather ships and stations had left their forecasting less precise than the Allies', who had realized that they would be able to squeak the landing on 6 June. Consequently, as Operation Overlord was launched, Rommel was on his way home to see his wife Lucie – whose birthday, as it happened, was 6 June.

PURPOSE SERVED?

Once battle was joined on D-Day, the Enigma data dried up to a considerable extent. The German Army, who were now the main opponent, avoided wireless communication where they could – not because they believed that Enigma had been compromised, but as a matter of good housekeeping: why take even the

Above: Coutances fell to Patton's troops during the 'breakout' from Normandy. His tanks had made short work of the well-thicketed and seemingly-impenetrable *bocage* country.

slightest risk of being overheard? Dug in along the coast, in fixed positions, they had well-established telephone communications; where they didn't, they used couriers on motorbikes and bicycles.

It hardly mattered now. D-Day itself was a day of action. Bletchley Park's main role, with the rest of Britain, was to sit back, wait and watch developments, while the Allied armed forces did their stuff. The codebreakers could afford to feel satisfaction at the support they had given the invasion of France, since its early planning stage, and to the Allied effort in the war at large.

Had Bletchley Park now served its purpose? It might have seemed that way, given how fast events were likely to unfold in the coming days and weeks. The great strategic chess game was over; Allied forces would be engaging with the Germans practically hand to hand. How much need would there be for the kind of intelligence the codebreakers could offer?

BREAKOUT

With Colossus now on stream and a staff of thousands turning round Enigma transcripts on arrival, Bletchley Park was coming close to being able to track developments in real time. This kind of material was to come into its own as Allied forces struggled to break out from the lodgement they had initially established in coastal Normandy.

ULTRA intelligence turned out to be of vital assistance to General Omar Bradley (1893–1981) and his First Army when they led the breakout in Operation Cobra (25–31 July). Intercepts had shown that the Germans had left one area of *bocage* country – mixed woods and hedged-off pastureland – only thinly protected on the assumption that the American Army would not be able to get through. They reckoned without the prongs or 'rhinoceros' tusks – sharp blades with which the Allied tanks were now equipped – that quickly carved a way through this countryside of thickets and small trees.

Below: US troops file through the streets of Laval, in the west of Normandy – far inland now, with the 'breakout' well under way.

Perhaps surprisingly, however, ULTRA intelligence was to be equally important to General Patton and his Third Army as, the worst of the static slugging over, they began advancing rapidly eastward and inland, and on towards the German homeland.

ULTRA-FAST

Patton's sense of urgency was only partly a product of his temperament. He wanted to follow through on the shock of Overlord. The confusion the invasion had caused had opened a window of opportunity for his Third Army and for the Allies in general: they needed to advance quickly before it closed. The

PRUDENT PATTON

HITLER PAID GEORGE S. Patton (1885–1945) an unintended compliment, calling him a 'crazy cowboy' of a general; for less jaundiced observers, he was 'daring', 'dashing' and 'freewheeling'. It wasn't really understood until recently that, apparently the most impetuous of attacking generals, Patton was actually being cautious, albeit at high speed.

It is true that Patton had little time for signals intelligence, as the cryptographer Arthur J. Levenson recalled years later. 'Patton, Patton didn't believe it,' he said:

And we got one message that said his headquarters was going to be strafed at a certain time. He said, 'Ha!' So he stood outside and then they came over and started shooting. He was a believer after that....

F.W. Winterbotham (1897–1990), in France with Patton in RAF intelligence, remembers how religiously he kept up with the latest briefings. He 'never failed to use every opportunity that ULTRA gave him to bust open the enemy', he said. Patton's daily ULTRA briefing – and the free-flowing discussion and debate it invariably occasioned – became his 'privy council', a staff member revealed.

That famous driving style arose out of meticulous preparation, Winterbotham argued – every apparently improvisatory twist and turn.

'Patton studied every ULTRA signal and, knowing where every enemy soldier was in his path, would thread his way round or through them and find the undefended spot. He had done it in Sicily and then all the way from Brittany to the Rhine.'

Where Patton *was* arguably incautious was in the recklessness with which he was prepared to share ULTRA information, well down the rankings – far below the levels officially allowed.

high speed of his advance depended on
the availability of ULTRA information
on the disposition, strength and state of
German forces where he was heading.

It was just as well that, retreating
rapidly now, their position changing
by the day and even by the hour, those
forces were newly reliant on wireless
communications. Bletchley Park noted
a sharp increase in ULTRA traffic
after the breakout in Normandy; the
resulting information went straight
back to Patton and his army.

On 1–2 August, for example,
panic-stricken signals from German
forces in Laval, in western France,
were intercepted. 'Supply columns to
be sent at once,' they said, calling for
transport 'for evacuation'. A few days
later, decrypted messages revealed
that 'withdrawal operations' were
'envisioned for night 5th/6th'. Acting on this information, US
forces were able to stroll into Laval next morning: they found the
little town completely clear.

Likewise, after a signal ordering the destruction of Rennes on
1 August was decrypted, the Allies could be fairly certain that the
city (although the capital of Brittany) was going to be abandoned
undefended. Again, US troops from the 8th Infantry Division
were able simply to saunter in and take possession.

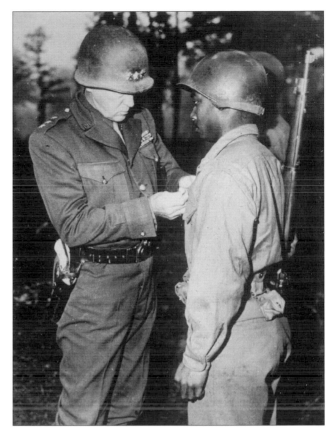

Above: A soldier's soldier,
driven and down-to-
earth, George S. Patton
discounted ULTRA
intelligence at first, but
quickly embraced it with
a convert's zeal.

HINDERED BY HITLER

Traffic from this time underlined for the Allies the extent to
which some of their enemy's most able commanders and toughest
troops were being thwarted by their *Führer*'s not-an-inch strategic
thinking. Hitler's orders were that his forces had to 'do everything
to hold St Malo' and other coastal strongholds. Another directive,
sent on 6 August, called for 'forces in Brittany to be concentrated

CULTURE CLASH

WE HAVE SEEN THAT the institutional culture at Bletchley Park was somewhat bohemian by the normal standards of the military. For the most part, this didn't matter too much. The codebreakers were tucked away in the English countryside, where their informal ways and casual style couldn't do much harm.

However, with the Allied invasion of Western Europe, when several signals staff were seconded to US Army units in France, these idiosyncratic attitudes could no longer be ignored. Well-drilled and disciplined officers winced to see the visitors' anarchic manner and slobbish self-presentation, as Lieutenant Colonel Melvin C. Helfers (1912–87) recalled:

They wore their uniforms as they pleased. They came and went as they pleased. They kept their quarters as they pleased and they cooked and ate as they pleased… Their intelligence was good but their attitude towards Americans was lousy as a rule.

in the fortresses of St Malo, Brest, Lorient and St Nazaire'. Patton took the hint and simply gave these places a swerve. Later, under interrogation, a captured German general was to describe what he called 'fortress mania' on his *Führer*'s part:

The enemy was content simply to keep these fortresses under observation, since they could do no harm to his conduct of the campaign as a whole. But they cost us between 160,000 and 200,000 men, together with costly weapons and equipment.

It was Hitler too who came up with the idea for Operation Lüttich – named (significantly) for a victory that the Germans had won during World War I. That one had been at Liège, Belgium: its return performance was supposed to be between Mortain and Avranches, in Normandy, where German forces had been struggling to hold on.

Thanks to Bletchley Park, the Allied Command was able to 'listen in' as Field Marshal Günther von Kluge (1882–1944), the experienced and capable commander on the ground, tried to talk Hitler out of his (quite crazy) plan for an immediate counteroffensive here.

'AVRANCHES, AVRANCHES!'

From the Allied point of view, the wrangling between Hitler and Von Kluge took on a soap opera quality. 'Everybody,' said F.W. Winterbotham, including Winston Churchill, 'was deeply involved in the Hitler–Kluge drama.' Reading these decrypted dispatches over the phone to Churchill, 'I sensed his controlled excitement at the other end.'

And not just because of the compelling human interest of the exchange; the quarrel seemed more significant than that, said Winterbotham: 'I think we all felt that this might well be the beginning of the end of the war.'

There was only one way this kind of argument between Hitler and one of his generals would end, of course. Bletchley Park was on hand to decrypt the direct order from the *Führer* when it came:

Attack on southern wing of Seventh Army will be conducted by Panzer Gruppe Eberbach after regrouping and bringing up of decisive offensive arms. On its success depends the fate of the battle of France.... Objective of the attack, the sea at Avranches

Below: Günther von Kluge with Hitler in happier times in 1943. The Führer's obduracy was ultimately to drive the Field Marshal to despair.

to which a bold and unhesitating thrust through is to be made. Rear attacking waves swinging north as opportunity occurs. ... Time of attack, probably on eleventh.

The detailed knowledge their decryptions gave them allowed the Allies to develop air–ground coordination of an unprecedented sophistication on an unprecedented scale. Patton called down fighter-bombers on the German units advancing from the east, while at the same time outflanking the Germans in the south, encircling them in the so-called 'Falaise Pocket'. Kluge's army was completely trounced: a subordinate last saw him 'tapping a map chart and moaning, "Avranches, Avranches! This town has cost me my reputation as a soldier."' The Field Marshal committed suicide not long after.

Below: German vehicles and bodies lie along a backroad in Normandy. Hitler's meddling made a bad situation worse. The roads around Falaise became a firing range for Allied artillery and fighter-bombers.

By 14 August, the Germans were scrambling to plug the
gaps in their defences. Fortunately, their frantic messages kept
Bletchley briefed on where these gaps were:

*Up to one Army into area south of Paris by quickest possible
means ... 64th Infantry not to be brought up to 19th Army, but
to area southeast Paris ... 15th Army, without awaiting arrival of
static divisions, to pull out 1st and then 2nd Infantry Divisions
and send them by quickest possible means to area south of Paris.*

UNDERSTANDING ULTRA

The Germans' own communications kept the Allies constantly
briefed, via Bletchley Park. Things were not as straightforward
as hindsight makes it seem, however, thanks to the need for

secrecy – and hence a degree of deception within Allied forces. Back in 1940, Air Chief Marshal Sir Hugh Dowding had been a martyr to this need for secrecy. As the war approached its end, the stakes were starting to seem lower. But the protection of the ULTRA secret still came at the cost of incomprehension – and, sometimes, exasperation – further down the hierarchy.

General Stafford LeRoy Irwin (1893–1955), at the head of the US Army's 5th Infantry Division in the drive across France, complained of the 'confusion in arrangements, transportation and plans' produced by sudden (and seemingly arbitrary) changes of mind by those above him. At times, it seemed, his orders 'made no sense at all' – although he was, ultimately, struck by the 'surprising absence of German opposition' that his force encountered.

Likewise, Major James D. Fellers (1913–97), ULTRA Representative to IX Tactical Air Command in Europe at this time, was asked by angry airmen why they were attacking empty space.

TOO GOOD TO BE TRUE?

'ULTRA WAS VERY ENTICING…', US cryptologist and career intelligence officer Brad Shwedo has observed: it seemed to give the military commander just about everything he could conceivably want. From 'exact order of battle strengths' and 'locations' to 'conditions of morale', it promised to take all the uncertainty out of waging war. Logistics messages, he points out, provided 'an interdiction playbook'; attack and movement orders quite literally told Allied commanders what their enemy was planning to do next.

As seductive as it was, that view was inevitably dangerous. ULTRA intelligence might never be 'wrong', but it could quite easily be misleading. As a May 1945 report by US intelligence officials found,

The raw intercepted messages themselves never give a complete or sequential chronicle; the gap must be filled by knowledge of the inner administration and operational procedures of the German armed forces and by deduction based on this knowledge. Often, ULTRA itself has been dangerously misleading. The ULTRA technique may decipher the message ordering an intended operation, but fail often to intercept the message that cancels or alters it.

Above: Outside the Air Ministry with Battle of Britain comrades, victory is bittersweet for Sir Hugh Dowding (centre), forced to 'celebrate' in civvies since his sacking.

Invariably, pilots would return from these missions reporting 'no aircraft seen' and somewhat 'browned off' at dumping their eggs on apparently inactive fields and dispersal areas.

Eventually, says Fellers:

…a IX pilot was shot down over one of the Angers strips and lay for days in the woods where he watched the German fighters take-off and land throughout the daylight hours and he observed their careful camouflage and dispersal systems. On his return to Allied lines he told of having been mentally gripped at the time of his attack because he could see no aircraft and thought he was performing a wasteful and useless mission. His eyewitness account did much to boost morale and obtain confidence in the advocated program.

But if there was a gap in comprehension on the Allied side, that was nothing by comparison with the complete bafflement of the Germans – a bafflement that the captured Field Marshal Gerd von Rundstedt expressed to his interrogators later. 'I would like to learn from you something,' he said. 'I don't understand how you could more or less be everywhere at once…'

If we were looking for the single statement that best summed up the codebreakers' contribution in the war, we would do well to find one more fitting than that.

APPENDIX: BLETCHLEY TODAY

Queen Elizabeth II has the reconstructed Bombe decoding machine explained to her by wartime operator Jane Valentine during a visit to Bletchley Park in July 2011.

SINCE 2014, WHEN IT was formally opened by HRH the Duchess of Cambridge, Bletchley Park's Block C has been a cleverly planned and beautifully fitted-out Visitor Centre, complete with café and gift shop and an exhibition about the Government Code and Cipher School's wartime work. Block C is really just an entrance-foyer, an introduction to the astonishing range of exhibits waiting to be seen across the site at large.

After a major grant from the National Lottery in 2011, the whole complex has been comprehensively refurbished. In the main 'Mansion' building you can see Alastair Denniston's office, and the old library where Naval Intelligence worked, pretty much as they must have been in 1940. Huts 3 and 6, where the codebreakers worked, have been restored to their former glory – or at least to their original shabby functionality. There's a sense of history here you can almost touch.

The Museum in Block B has the world's only reconstructed Bombe, assorted Enigma machines and exhibits on everything from the Lorenz machine to the life of Alan Turing. The office he worked in can be seen in Hut 8, while in Hut 11 you can see where an army of Wrens manned the Bombes around the clock.

BIBLIOGRAPHY

Aldrich, Richard J. *Intelligence and the War Against Japan: Britain, America and the Politics of Secret Service.* Cambridge: CUP, 2000.

Batey, Mavis. *Dilly: The Man Who Broke Enigmas.* London: Biteback, 2010.

Copeland, B. Jack (ed.), *Colossus: The Secrets of Bletchley Park's Codebreaking Computers.* Oxford: OUP, 2010.

Dunlop, Tessa. *The Bletchley Girls: War, Secrecy, Love and Loss: The Women of Bletchley Park Tell Their Story.* London: Hodder & Stoughton, 2015.

Harper, Glyn. *The Battle for North Africa: El Alamein and the Turning Point for World War II.* Bloomington: Indiana University Press, 2017.

Hinsley, F.H. and Stripp, Alan (eds.). *Codebreakers: The Inside Story of Bletchley Park.* Oxford: OUP, 1993.

Lewin, Ronald. *Ultra Goes to War.* Barnsley: Pen & Sword, 2008.

Llewelyn-Jones, Malcolm. *The Royal Navy and the Arctic Convoys: A Naval Staff History.* London: Routledge, 2013.

Mann, C. *British Policy and Strategy Towards Norway, 1941–45.* New York: Springer, 2012.

Mann, Chris and Jörgenson, Christer. *Hitler's Arctic War: The German Campaigns in Norway, Finland and the USSR.* Barnsley: Pen & Sword, 2016.

McKay, Sinclair. *The Secret Life of Bletchley Park: The History of the Wartime Codebreaking Centre and the Men and Women who were There.* London: Aurum, 2010.

Nesbit, Roy Conyers. *Ultra Versus U-Boats: Enigma Decrypts in the National Archives.* Barnsley: Pen & Sword, 2008.

Roberts, Jerry. *Lorenz: Breaking Hitler's Top-Secret Code at Bletchley Park.* Stroud: History Press, 2017.

Russell-Jones, Mair. *My Secret Life in Hut Six: One Woman's Experiences at Bletchley Park.* Oxford: Lion, 2014.

Sangster, Andrew. *Field Marshal Kesselring: Great Commander or War Criminal.* Newcastle upon Tyne: Cambridge Scholars Publishing, 2015.

Sebag-Montefiore, Hugh. *Enigma: The Battle for the Code.* London: Weidenfeld & Nicolson, 2000.

Shwedo, Bradford J. *XIX Tactical Command and ULTRA: Patton's Force Enhancers in the 1944 Campaign in France.* Maxwell AFB, AL: Air University Press, 2012.

Smith, Christopher. *The Hidden History of Bletchley Park: A Social and Organisational History, 1939–1945.* London: Palgrave, 2015.

INDEX